Book one in the

CIRCLE OF MAGIC

quartet

THE MAGIC IN THE WEAVING

Also by Tamora Pierce:

The Song of the Lioness Quartet

1. Alanna: The First Adventure
2. In the Hand of the Goddess
3. The Woman Who Rides Like a Man
4. Lioness Rampant

Look out for:

The Immortals

1. Wild Magic
2. Wolf-Speaker
3. The Emperor Mage
4. Realms of the Gods

Circle of Magic

2. The Power in the Storm
3. The Fire in the Forging
4. The Healing in the Vine

Point

TAMORA PIERCE

CIRCLE OF MAGIC

THE MAGIC IN THE WEAVING

Scholastic Children's Books,
Commonwealth House, 1-19 New Oxford Street,
London WC1A 1NU, UK
a division of Scholastic Ltd
London ~ New York ~ Toronto ~ Sydney ~ Auckland
Mexico City ~ New Delhi ~ Hong Kong

First published in hardback in the US by Scholastic Inc, 1998
First published in the UK by Scholastic Ltd, 1998
This edition published in the UK by Scholastic Ltd, 1999

ISBN 0 439 01426 3

Typeset by DP Photosetting, Aylesbury, Bucks.
Printed and bound in Great Britain
by Mackays of Chatham plc, Chatham, Kent

10 9 8 7 6 5 4 3 2 1

To Gwen E. Meeks,
who gave me the original working title of this book,
without which I could not have written it –
may your writing be as rewarding for you
as mine has been for me

ACKNOWLEDGEMENTS

My most heartfelt thanks to David Fickling, Julia Moffatt, Kirsten Skidmore, and the wonderful staff of Scholastic Ltd. I deeply appreciate all you've done for me in publishing my books throughout the British Commonwealth and look forward to working with you in the future.

My thanks also go to my mother, Mary Lou Pierce, who gave me the benefit of her experience in gardening, to Victorian Video for their drop spindle package and instructional spinning videotape, to Richard McCaffery Robinson, whose aid on the maps and on the cultural background of the *Circle* world has been invaluable, and to Thomas Gansevoort, whose tales of his work in many different crafts inspired this series.

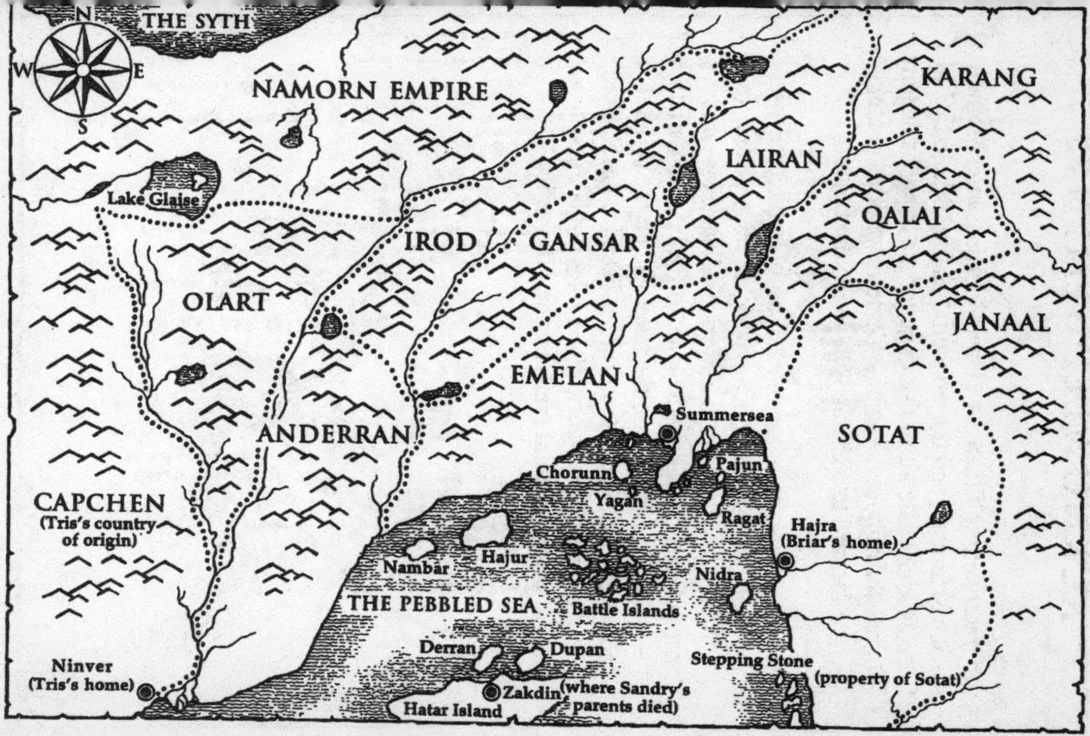
N
W
E
S
THE SYTH
NAMORN EMPIRE
KARANG
LAIRAN
QALAI
Lake Glaise
IROD
GANSAR
OLART
JANAAL
EMELAN
Summersea
ANDERRAN
SOTAT
Chorunn
Pajun
Yagan
CAPCHEN
(Tris's country
of origin)
Ragat
Hajra
(Briar's home)
Nambar
Hajur
Nidra
THE PEBBLED SEA
Battle Islands
Derran
Dupan
Stepping Stone
Ninver
(Tris's home)
(property of Sotat)
Zakdin
(where Sandry's
parents died)
Hatar Island

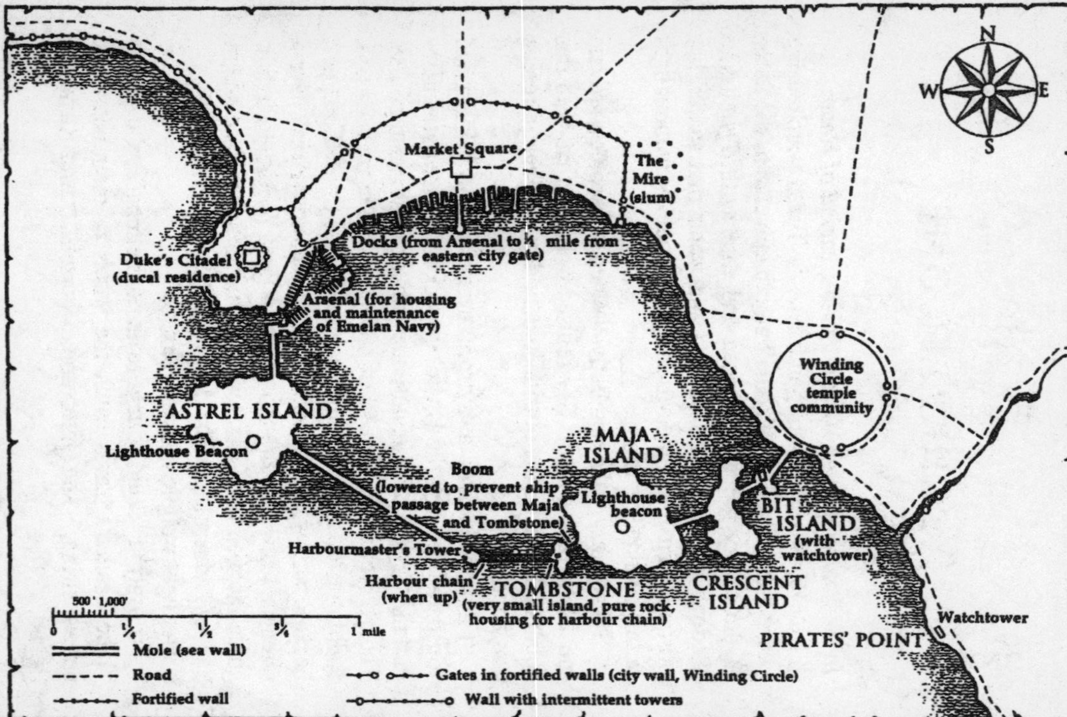
N
W
E
S
Market Square
The Mire (slum)
Docks (from Arsenal to ¼ mile from eastern city gate)
Duke's Citadel (ducal residence)
Arsenal (for housing and maintenance of Emelan Navy)
Winding Circle temple community
ASTREL ISLAND
Lighthouse Beacon
MAJA ISLAND
Boom (lowered to prevent ship passage between Maja and Tombstone)
Lighthouse beacon
BIT ISLAND (with watchtower)
Harbourmaster's Tower
Harbour chain (when up)
TOMBSTONE (very small island, pure rock, housing for harbour chain)
CRESCENT ISLAND
Watchtower
PIRATES' POINT
500' 1,000'
0 ¼ ½ ¾ 1 mile
Mole (sea wall)
Road
Fortified wall
Gates in fortified walls (city wall, Winding Circle)
Wall with intermittent towers

CHAPTER ONE

In the Palace of Black Swans, Zakdin, capital of Hatar:

Blue eyes wide, Lady Sandrilene fa Toren watched her near-empty oil lamp. Her small mouth quivered as the flame at the end of the wick danced and shrank, throwing grim shadows on the barrels of food and water that shared her prison. When that flame was gone, she would be without light in this windowless room.

"I'll go crazy," she said flatly. "When they come to rescue me, I'll be raving mad." She refused to admit that, with this room locked from the outside and hidden by magic, a rescue was hopeless.

"I'll draw the mob away from here, far away," Pirisi had whispered through the keyhole, speaking in her native Tradertalk. "You'll be safe, until the smallpox has run its course. Then I'll return for you." But her nurse had never returned. Right outside the door, the mob had caught and killed her, because she was a Trader. Sandry, hearing Pirisi's dying screams, knew that she too was now dead. Without Pirisi to guide them to her, no rescuers would find the place where Sandry had spent her last days.

Her light wobbled, and shrank.

"If only I could *catch* it in something!" she cried. "Like Trader wizards catch the winds in their nets— A net is string," she interrupted herself. "And string is thread..."

She had thread, in the workbasket she had grabbed when Pirisi dragged her from her room. The basket's contents had kept her from giving up completely before this, as she embroidered until her eyes refused to focus. She had thread a-plenty, in coils and in her work.

"I'm no mage," she argued, resting her head on one hand. "I'm just a girl – a *noble* girl, worse yet. Like that maid said, 'Good f'r naught but to be waited on and to marry.' Good-for-naught, that's me..."

Tears filled her eyes, making the lamp flame quiver even more.

"Crying won't help!" she snapped. "I have to do *something*! Something besides weep and talk to myself!" She dragged her workbasket over. Fumbling, she yanked out three coils of silk, one green, one pale grey, one bright red. Swiftly, she arranged them: one in her lap, one to her left, one to her right.

The light was down to a blue core and its wavering orange skirt.

Gathering the ends of the threads in her left hand, she pulled them together in a knot, tying it as snugly as she could. Finding long dressmaker's pins in her basket, she pinned the knot to a barrel to anchor it. Her fingers shook; sweat crawled down her face. She didn't want to think of what would happen if this didn't work.

Worse, there was no reason for it *to* work. Pirisi, the Trader and servant, had magic. Lady Sandrilene fa Toren was good only to be waited on and to marry.

"Nothing to lose," she said, and took a deep breath. "Nothing at all." Aboard the Trader-ships their *mimanders* – mages – called to the winds as if they were friends who could be invited to stay. "Come on," she told the dying flame.

"Come here, won't you? You'll last in these threads longer than you will in that lamp."

That lamp guttered. The flame was gobbling the few drops of oil that remained in its bowl.

The girl started her braid. The green thread wrapped around her fingers like a strangling vine. The grey slithered to the floor like a snake. The red tangled with itself.

"*Uvumi* – patience. It is everything," Pirisi had often told Sandry. "Without patience magic would be undiscovered – in rushing everything, we would never hear its whisper inside."

"*Uvumi*," Sandry whispered in Tradertalk. She straightened the threads, one on each side, one in her lap. Closing her eyes, she found that she was much calmer when she couldn't see her work or the lamp. She didn't really *need* to see, to do something as easy as a braid. In her mind, her threads gleamed brightly. They called specks of light from all around her, and tangled them in their strands.

The flickering lamp went out; she opened her eyes. The wick was dead and black. Through and around her braid, light shone steadily, filling the room with a soft, pearly glow.

"Did I know I could do that?" she whispered.

The braid-light wavered.

"All right," she said, gathering the threads once more. "But I have to sleep, you know." She wiped her eyes on her sleeve. With a whispered "*Uvumi*," Sandrilene fa Toren went back to work.

In the southeastern Pebbled Sea:

When she sat up, and looked at herself, Daja thought she was a ghost. Her skin was all sparkly white. Had an enemy *mimander* turned her from a brown Trader into a white one? Why on earth would anyone do such a thing?

She ran her swollen tongue over cracked lips, tasted salt, and grimaced at her own foolishness. This was no *mimander*'s doing. It was what happened when a sea-soaked girl fell asleep, and didn't wake until the sun was high overhead. She brushed herself off, salt flakes dropping on to her makeshift raft. White grains got into her many cuts and scrapes, where they burned like fire.

Her family ship was gone, sunk in a storm that their *mimander* could not stop or get rid of. The Trader god, Koma, known for peculiar acts, had chosen Daja to be the only one left alive, floating on a square wooden hatch-cover.

All around her lay a spreading pool of wreckage. She saw tangles of rope and wood, shattered crates, smears of colour that were precious dyes from their cargo. Bodies also drifted there, the silent remains of her family. Daja's lips trembled. How long would it be until she joined them? Should she jump into the water now and end it? Drowning was quicker than starvation.

Something thumped nearby: an open leather chest slammed against a mast. Again it thumped against the wood as water swelled, then flattened beneath it. She could just glimpse its contents, some bundles and dark glass bottles. It was what Traders called a *suraku* – a survival box. They were kept everywhere on the ships. She had to get it, and she prayed that its contents weren't soaked or ruined.

Daja reached out. The box was beyond her grasp. She looked around for a long piece of wood to grab it with – no luck. Water surged in another slow roll, and her raft moved away from the wreckage. The box stayed behind.

"No!" she cried. "No!" She strained to grab that precious thing, though yards now lay between her and it. "Come here! Come on, I – I *order* you!" She half-laughed, half-cried to hear such foolishness. "Come on," she whispered, as she had coaxed the ship's dogs to come to their food bowls. She was not very old, after all – she did not want to die. Tears rolling down her cheeks, she reached out, and twitched her fingers as if she beckoned to her pets.

Later she would wonder if she had just imagined it, being crazy with the sun and terrified of death. Now she stared, jaw dropping, as the box pulled away from the mast, and floated towards her. It stopped twice along the way. Both times she wiggled her fingers, afraid to move anything else. Both times the box came forward, until it bumped her hand.

Very, very carefully, she drew her prize on to the hatch-cover. It was indeed a *suraku*, lined with copper to keep the damp out and life in. The bundles were oiled cloth, to keep their contents dry. The corks in the bottles had wax seals. Gently she felt through everything, and grabbed a bottle. It took nearly all her strength to wriggle the cork out. When it popped free, liquid sprayed on to her face. Fresh water! Greedily, she drank most of that bottle before she came to her senses. If she guzzled it all now, there would be less for tomorrow. She had to save it. She fumbled to put the cork back in. Inspecting the other bottles, she saw they also held water.

"Thank you, Trader Koma," she whispered to the god of deals and rewards.

In the bundles she found cheese, bread, apples. She ate carefully, in tiny bites, as her lips cracked open and bled. All thought of the future had vanished; for right now, she was gloriously *alive*.

The *suraku* lasted for three days, and might have kept her for two more, if she ate less than ever. In all that time, she saw no sign of ships. It was early in the trading season –

captains more cautious than her mother were still in port.

Knowing her food was nearly gone, she tried to strike a deal with Koma and his wife, Bookkeeper Oti. "I don't look like much now," she told them, her voice only a thin croak, "but I'm a better deal than you think! I'm strong, I know most seaman's knots – except maybe the pinned sheepshank, but I'll work on that." She bit her lip. She didn't dare cry – it would mean losing water, with none to replace it.

Far away, so far that it didn't seem real, she heard the crack of canvas. Was it a dream? Slowly, she turned her head. She was in the trench of a swell – all she could see were the peaks of water on either side.

Her nostrils flared. The wind blew as the trench she was in rose and flattened. New smells drifted into her nose. Breathing deep, she recognized the dull odour of brass, riding on the back of the rusty tang of iron.

Metal meant people – didn't it? Metal – except for the bands on her raft, and in the box at her side – went straight to the bottom without a ship to hold it up.

"Ahoy!" A man's voice sounded over the water. "Ahoy! Are you alive?"

"Yes!" Daja cried. She kept a hand on her beautiful *sur-aku*. The other she stretched as high as she dared, and waved carefully. If she fell in now, she was far too weak to swim.

She lost track of time. It seemed like for ever until she heard the splash of oars, and saw a longboat come alongside. In its bow sat a lean white man. His large, dark eyes were set deep under thick brows and a heavy fringe of black lashes. He wore long, silver and black hair tied back. A Trader to the bone, she noted that his yellow shirt and grey breeches were linen and well-made, not a sailor's usual cheap wool.

"Hello, there," he said, as casually as if they'd met at the marketplace. "My name is Niko – Niklaren – Goldeye. I've been looking for you. I'm sorry not to have found you sooner." As sailors guided the boat closer, he reached for Daja, and pulled her into the boat. Someone held a flask of water to her lips.

"Wait!" she cried, voice rasping, as she fought to sit up. "My – my box! There!" She pointed. "Please – save it!"

The sailors looked at Niko, who nodded. Only when they had brought the chest into the boat, and stowed it next to her, did she relax and drink their water.

In Hajra, port city of Sotat:

The first time the Hajran street guard caught Roach with a hand on someone else's purse, they tattooed an X on the web of skin between right thumb and forefinger, then tossed him into a big holding cell overnight. Nursing his sore hand, Roach went straight to the far edge of the chamber, where a watery beam of sunshine reached down from an opening in the wall. Patches of cushiony moss grew there. Sitting on the floor, Roach found that one of them made a fine pillow.

Months later, a shopkeeper grabbed Roach as the boy helped himself to a few scarves. The guard took him, tattooed an X on the web of his left hand, and tossed him into the same holding cell. The moss had grown to cover a whole corner. It made a soft couch where he could sleep and wait to be released in the morning.

Roach's current visit was his third; the guard had nabbed his entire gang of street rats in a jeweller's shop. Most of them already had two X tattoos, which meant they got no third release from justice. All of them were thrown into the great holding cell. His moss now covered the entire corner, and a good amount of floor as well. It was the most comfortable bed that he'd ever had, with room left over for the rest of his gang-mates to use it for a pillow.

As others scrambled for a share of the slop the guard called supper, Roach whispered to his moss. "I won't be back," he explained. "Third time's cursed. I'll get the mines, or galleys, or shipyards. 'Less I break out, it's for life." He smiled faintly. Life was a short thing now. No one lived more than two years in those places, and escapes were rare.

For all that, he slept well. When he woke, it was Judging Day in Hajra, and the guard had come for him.

"Weevil," brayed a guard at the door. Roach's gang-mates sat up. "Dancer. Alleycat. Viper. Slug." Roach hissed angrily. It was Slug that got them all in this fix, watching them steal instead of looking out for street guards. "Cheater. Turtle. Roach."

Roach hesitated. Should he make them come get him?

A guard cracked a whip, looking at him. Roach decided to avoid the beating he'd get if the man had to drag him. With two Xs on his hands, he'd receive plenty of beatings in the future as it was. "Thank you," he told the moss, and joined the rest of his gang.

They were quick-marched past other cells, then up a long flight of stairs. On the level floors, the guard began to trot, urging the captives along with their whips. Roach was gasping when they were driven into a huge, echoing chamber.

A woman in the grey robes of a magistrate sat behind a long table. People in street clothes stood behind her. Clerks sat on each end of the table; they scribbled as guards and civilians testified against criminals. Roach ignored the testimony that concerned his gang. These grand folk had already judged him, so why listen to their cackle?

When the testimony was done, a clerk called out,

"Weevil." The gang leader was shoved in front of the judge.

"Hands," she ordered. The guards slammed Weevil's hands down on the table, holding them so the X-shaped tattoos were visible. Like Roach, Weevil had two of them.

"Mines," the judge said. A guard shoved Weevil into a wooden holding pen at the rear of the chamber.

Roach shut out the rest as the law officers worked their way through the gang. Instead he thought of those plants in the cell, how peacefully green the moss showed when even a tiny bit of sun touched it. Give him a green like that from a living plant over the light that danced in emeralds. That was hard colour; the moss-glow was soft. The plant didn't seem to need much earth to grow in, though it liked water. He'd given it part of his water ration when no one was looking. He didn't mind being good to growing things, but he did object when others made fun of him for doing it.

Twin pairs of rough hands picked him up, then dropped him in front of the magistrate's table, jarring his ankles. He growled and fought as the guards dragged his hands out in front of him. He knew it was useless, but he didn't care – they'd remember him, at least!

The judge didn't look at his face, only his hands. "Docks," she said, and yawned.

They were dragging Roach to a separate pen from the one which held Weevil and Viper when a light male voice said, "A moment."

It was not a request, but a command. The guards looked back. Roach did not.

"May I see the boy again?" the man enquired.

"Bring him." The judge sounded bored.

Roach was hauled back to stand in front of a civilian. This was no lawyer or soldier. His long, loose over-robe was a deep blue, dyed cloth that cost a silver penny the yard on Draper's Lane. It was worn open over loose grey breeches, a pale grey shirt and good boots. He carried only a dagger; it hung next to the purse on his belt.

This was a Money-Bag, then, or an officer. Somebody big, for certain. Somebody who wore power like a cloak.

The Bag whispered to the judge, who made a face. He held something before her eyes, a letter with a beribboned seal on it. The judge glared at Roach, but nodded, and the Bag stepped away from her. "Their Majesties are inclined to mercy, as you are but a youth." The judge rattled it off fast, a speech learned by heart. "You have a choice – the docks, or exile from Sotat and service at the..." She faltered.

The Bag bent down to whisper, long, grey-streaked black hair tumbling forward to hide his face. Roach wondered if he was looking for a cute little servant boy, and grinned. Men who liked play-toys always regretted meeting him.

The man straightened, and looked around until his dark eyes caught and held Roach's grey-green ones. There was something in that black gaze, something that had nothing to do with human toys. Roach's sense of power held in check grew threefold when he met those eyes. They warned – and comforted – at the same time.

Roach looked down.

"You have a choice of the docks, or apprenticeship to the Winding Circle Temple in Emelan," the judge went on, "until you take formal vows at the temple, or until its governing council rules that you are fit to enter society. Temple or docks, boy. Choose."

Choose? There were guards on the docks, nasty, wary fellows. What temple could hang on to a smart rat like him? Better yet, Emelan was far to the north of Sotat, fresh territory where no one knew who he was. "Temple," he replied.

"Make out transfer papers," the judge told a clerk. "Master Niklaren" – this was to the blue-robed man – "will you take charge of him?"

"Of course."

For a moment Roach's heart raced; he might be able to run before he ever saw Emelan! Then he met the Bag's eyes, and gave up that idea. The man – Master Niklaren? – looked too wise to fall for any dodge he might pull.

"I can't make out papers for a 'roach'," whined the clerk. "Not to a *temple.*"

"This is a chance, lad." Niklaren's voice was light in tone for a man's. "You can pick a name, one that's yours alone. You can choose how you will be seen from now on."

Only as long as I stay, Roach thought. Still, the Bag was right. Roach had never liked his name, but no one argued with the title the Thief-Lord gave.

"Choose, boy, and hurry up," snapped the judge. "I've other cases besides yours."

The docks were too close to risk annoying these people. What name would temple folk like? Plant and animal names, that was it. He imagined robed men and women smiling at him and giving up the key to the temple gate.

Plant and animal names. A picture flashed into his mind: a green, velvet corner – but that wouldn't do. He needed a tough name, one that would tell folk he was not to be trifled with. He studied his hands, trying to think – and noticed scarred welts across his right palm, a souvenir of a vine that grew on a merchant's garden wall.

"What's them vines with needles on them? Big, sharp ones, that rip chunks out when you grab 'em?"

The Bag smiled. "Roses. Briars."

He liked the sound of that second one. "Briar, then."

"You need a last name," the clerk said, rolling his eyes.

A last name? wondered Roach. *Whatever for?*

The judge tapped the desk impatiently.

"Moss," he said. No one would think he was moss-soft if he just didn't use it.

"Briar Moss," said the clerk, and filled in the blank space on his paper. "Master Niko, I'll need your signature."

Briar frowned. "Master" was a word for professors, judges and wizards. The temples called men and women "Dedicate". Who was this man, anyway?

"Cut him loose," the Bag – Master Niklaren – ordered the guards.

"Your pardon, sir, but you don't know what he's like!" growled one of them. "He's born and bred to vice—"

Niklaren straightened, and caught the man with those black, powerful eyes. "Are these remarks addressed to me?"

Roach shivered – was the room suddenly colder? The judge drew a circle of protection on the front of her robe. The guard's face went as white as milk. His partner cut Roach free.

"Briar won't run – will you, lad?" Niklaren bent to sign the clerk's paper. Briar/Roach sensed that the Bag was right. Something about this man made escape seem like a bad idea.

I'll stick till we get to this temple place, he told himself. *I can get lost there, easy*.

In the city of Ninver, in Capchen:

In the darkness of the temple dormitory, when she was trying to cry herself to sleep with the least amount of noise, Trisana Chandler heard voices. It wasn't the first time that she'd done so, but these voices were different. This time she could identify the speakers. They sounded exactly like the girls who shared the dormitory with her.

"I heard her very own *parents* brought her here, and dropped her off, and said they never wanted to see her again."

Tris was sure about that one: it was the girl in the bed on her right, the one who had tried to shove ahead of her in the line for the dining hall. Tris had raised a fuss, and a Dedicate had sent the girl to the back of the line.

"*I* heard they passed her from relative to relative, until there weren't any who wanted her any more."

Tris yanked at one of the coppery curls that had jumped out of her night-time braid. She was fairly certain about this speaker, too: the girl whose bed was across the room and two more beds to her left. She had tried to copy Tris's answers to a mathematics question just that morning. The moment Tris had realized what was going on, she had covered her slate: she despised people who copied.

"Have you seen her *clothes*? Those ugly dresses! That black wool's so old it's turning brown!"

"And they strain at the seams. Fat as she is, you'd think she'd eat more at table!"

She wasn't completely sure about the last speakers, but did it matter? The voices seemed to come from every bed in the dormitory, to cut at her like razors. Why did they do this, the ones she'd never even spoken to? Because it felt good to be mean with no one to see and blame them? Because it felt good to sneer as the group did, go after the targets that their leaders pointed out? Her cousins were the same, following those who loved to make fun of the outcast among them, like ducklings chasing their mother.

When her parents had given her to the Dedicate Superior of Stone Circle, she had thought she'd run out of hurt feelings. It seemed that she hadn't, after all.

Tris clenched her hands in her sheets. *Leave me* alone, she thought, speechless with fury and shame. *I never did* anything *to most of you, don't even* know *most of you...*

No one noticed that the wind had picked up, jerking at the shutters on the windows, making them clack against their fittings.

"I bet her parents tried to sell her to Traders."

"Maybe, but even Traders wouldn't take her. They wouldn't think she has value!"

Everyone found this hilarious.

One of the shutters hadn't been securely locked. It burst open, letting in a swirl of cold wind. The girls nearest to it screamed and jumped to close it. A gust of wind bowled them on to their rumps before it whipped around the room, pulling covers off beds, scouring belongings off the small shelves. By the time it roared out of the room, all of the girls but one were screaming.

Two dedicates, their habits thrown on over their nightgowns, rushed into the room, carrying lamps. Everywhere they looked, there was a chaos of bedding, girls and knick-knacks – except at Tris's bed. It was untouched. The girl in it stared at them with tear-reddened, defiant eyes behind the brass-rimmed spectacles that she had just finished jamming on to her long nose.

The next morning, after breakfast, they brought her down to the office of Stone Circle's Dedicate Superior, and left her in the waiting room. Beside her they placed her few bags, completely packed. She had not said a word. There was no point in it, and by now she knew how stupid it was to try to talk to someone who was determined to get rid of her.

As she waited, staring fixedly at those battered leather satchels, she realized that the Honoured Dedicate's door was not quite closed.

"...I know that you're already on your way to Winding Circle, and I need you to take this girl with you. Is that such a hard request to grant, Master Niko?"

"Send her later in the spring, when the trade caravans leave for Emelan." The light, crisp, male voice sounded annoyed. "I'm on a very special task these days. If I have to change my plans suddenly, this child will only get in my way."

"We can't keep her. Her parents swore that she was tested for magic and found to have none, but..." The Dedicate Superior's voice trailed off. Briskly she continued, "I don't know if she's possessed by a spirit, or part elemental, or carrying a ghost, to be at the centre of such uproar, and I don't care. Winding Circle is far better equipped to handle a case like hers. They have the learning, and dedicates who are more open-minded with regard to unique cases. They have the best mages south of your own university. They will know what to do with her."

Hearing all this, Tris felt sick. Spirit, elemental or ghost-burdened, was she? And what kind of fate awaited her? Some people learned to manage such creatures within themselves; others got rid of them. Far too many ended up homeless and crazy, wandering the streets, or locked up in an attic or cellar, or even dead. She swayed, feeling ill – and then clenched her fists. She was sick of it! Sick of being gotten rid of, sick of being discussed, sick of not being helped. Whatever was wrong with her, whatever made her so undesirable to keep around, it was *not her fault*!

With a thundering roar, hailstones battered the roof and

walls around her, hitting wood and stone like a multitude of hammers. They shattered the glass panes of the window in the outer office to spray across the floor like icy diamonds. Clumsily she knelt, to pick up a handful.

The door of the Dedicate Superior's office swung open, revealing a slender man in his middle fifties. He stood there, hands on hips, black eyes under thick black brows fixed on Tris.

From the floor she glared at him, hailstones trickling from her fingers. "It's not polite to stare," she snapped, not over her fury.

"You were tested for magic?" he asked, his clipped voice abrupt.

Why did this stranger taunt her? Her family would have put up with her oddities if only she'd been proved to have magic, which might be turned to the profit of House Chandler. "By the most expensive mage in Ninver, if you *must* know. And *he* said I haven't a speck of it."

The stranger turned, and looked at the woman in the yellow habit behind him. "Honoured Wrenswing, I've changed my mind. I will be very happy to escort Trisana Chandler to Winding Circle Temple in Emelan." He smiled thinly, and reached a hand to Tris. "I am pleased to meet you, young lady."

She ignored the outstretched hand. Getting up, she shook out her skirts. "You'll change your mind before long," she retorted. "Everyone does."

In the storeroom:

Carefully Sandry eyed her right-most thread. There was the knot that she'd tied close to the end. "Time to put in something new," she told the waiting darkness with a sigh.

She was all out of green now. It had given her good service, glowing with a clearer light than either the grey or the red. She would miss it.

Yards of braid lay in a coil from which she continued to work. She fixed her mind on it and on light completely, except for the times that she ate, or slept, or used the stinking barrel that was her chamberpot. Keeping light in her threads took all of her attention, leaving her without time or energy for panic.

She groped behind her for her workbasket, and froze. Muffled voices cried out on the other side of the wall.

The girl swallowed hard. Had things gotten this bad? Was she going to start imagining people when they were not there?

"This way, dolts!" a voice cried.

"...don't see anything!" someone, a man, growled in the distance.

The light in her braid paled. "Don't you *dare*," she ordered in a whisper. She couldn't keep her mind on it. The glow died.

Breathless, she waited in the dark. If this was a dream, she wished it would stop!

"You *won't* see anything," a crisp, educated voice snapped. Its owner might have been in the same room with her – or on the other side of the door. "It was spelled for concealment."

She clapped her hands over her mouth and started to rock. *This is it*, she thought, *I've gone mad at last.*

Something entered the room, a rush of cool air that wasn't really air, a feeling of water more than a breeze. Most of it circled over the empty sacks she used for a bed. A lone thread spun out of that cool mass. Drifting across the room, it twined around her shoulders.

"*Now* do you see it?" the educated voice demanded. "I want the locksmith."

"You've got 'im, Master Niko." That deep voice also sounded very close.

Metal scraped on metal. Air moved. She didn't know that the door was opening until it bumped her.

"Urda bless me, what a stink!" the deep voice said.

"Move aside, man," the crisp voice ordered. Its owner, a light-coloured shadow, stepped into the room. "My child? My name is Niklaren Goldeye. I've been looking for you." He raised a lamp that someone had passed to him.

The light struck her eyes, which had been in the gloom so long. Pain made her scream, and cover them. She would see almost nothing for quite some time.

CHAPTER TWO

Summersea, in Emelan:

Sandry's great-uncle, Duke Vedris IV, ruler of Emelan, watched the rain fall outside the library window as first Niko, then Sandry, told the tale of the last four months, of Sandry's rescue, healing, and the long trip north. If he had opinions about their tale, they were locked behind his deep-set brown eyes and heavy features. Stocky, broad-shouldered and commanding, the Duke preferred simple clothes like those he had on: a white lawn shirt, brown wool breeches, a brown wool over-tunic and calf-high boots. Only the flash of gold braid at his tunic collar and hems, and the signet ring on his left forefinger, hinted that he might be wealthy. With his shaved head, hooked nose and fleshy visage, the Duke looked like one of his own pirate-chasing captains, rather than a nobleman whose line had ruled from this castle for eight hundred years.

When they finished, he turned to look at them. "Master Niko, it was good of you to bring Sandrilene to me, particularly at this time of year."

"The land roads weren't so bad, your Grace," replied Niko, stirring his tea. "And certainly I couldn't abandon Sandry at that point."

"I know I should have waited till spring, Uncle," the girl added, "but I just couldn't. Hatar – it's a giant graveyard now. I couldn't stay an hour more." She was still pale and thin after her ordeal in the cellar and weeks of recovery. Dressed in black from head to toe, she had become a small ghost. Niko's suggestion, to bring her north to her father's favourite relative, had been welcome.

Vedris smiled. "I understand, my dear. You don't have to apologize."

Sandry returned the smile with a small, trembling one of her own.

The Duke sighed, and rubbed his shaved scalp. "You have presented me with a dilemma, however, if you want to stay," he said regretfully. His voice was the most elegant thing about him, smooth and velvet-soft, the kind of voice that others fell silent to hear. "Do you wish to remain? Or do you want to head north in the spring?"

Sandry shook her head, making the twin braids fly. "I don't want to go to Namorn, if you please, Uncle."

The Duke sat in the window seat. "After my lady wife died, I let court functions go. My nobles socialize with one another at their homes. With no hostess, and my children all grown and married, there is no lady here I would like to ask to take you under her wing. You are welcome to stay as long as you desire, but this castle is a grim place for a young girl to grow up in."

Sandry looked down at her lap. The picture he painted was not appealing. The thought of days in these plain stone halls was a lonely one. The idea of packing and travelling to distant Namorn, at any season of the year, sounded far worse. She hadn't *liked* her Namornese relatives.

"Then I have the solution," Niko said cheerfully. "I'm surprised you didn't see it yourself, your Grace. Lady Sandrilene can live at Winding Circle Temple. Your nobles send their own children there. She can learn the things that she will need to move in society, and she will get an education worth having." Looking at Sandry, he explained, "Winding Circle is known throughout the Pebbled Sea as a centre of learning and magic."

Magic? Sandry thought, wistfully. She had thought the magic in the world died with Pirisi. "I'd like to see magic again," she whispered.

"It *is* the obvious solution," Niko told the Duke, who looked at him sharply. "She will be close by, as safe behind those walls as she might be here. The two of you can visit whenever you like."

"Sandrilene?" asked the Duke.

She smiled tiredly. "I don't know, Uncle, but – surely it's worth a try?"

Nidra Island, off the shore of Sotat:

It had taken so little time for her to tell the Trader Council of the fate of Third Ship Kisubo, out early to get in a fast cargo, sunk in a late winter storm. The five judges – two land-Traders, two sea-Traders, and a *mimander* – retired when she finished, to discuss her fate. In the judging-room, Daja and her rescuer waited for their verdict.

Daja was sick with hope: they might let her live among those of her relatives who were too old or too young for the hard life at sea, at one of the Traders' handful of hidden cities. They might give her a new name, send her to a new family. People had gotten second chances like that – rarely, but it happened.

"Prepare yourself for the worst," advised Niko, his eyes kind. "You know they regard lone survivors as the worst kind of luck."

Daja shook her head. It wasn't that she didn't believe him.

She simply didn't want to admit that he might be right.

The door opened; the members of the Council filed in. One, a woman, carried the bulky logbook, in which the names of all Trader families, vessels and companies were recorded. Placing it on the judges' table, she opened it, leafing through the pages, until she reached the one she sought.

Over his – or her – arms (Daja couldn't tell the sex of the person in those bulky robes and veils), the *mimander* carried a staff. Like any Trader's staff, it was five feet long and made of ebony, a symbol of pride and of a Trader's right to protect himself. Brass caps on both ends guarded them from wear and tear. The cap on every other staff in the room bore designs of engravings, bumps and inlaid wire. On this staff, the cap was unmarked.

Seeing it, Daja began to shiver. An unmarked staff meant only one thing.

"As in the days when our people first carried fire, weaving and metal-work to the non-Traders, the *kaqs*," said the chief judge, a man, "so it is now. Daja Kisubo, lone survivor of disaster, we declare you to be outcast, the worst kind of bad luck, *trangshi*. As *trangshi* you must bear this staff always..."

The *mimander* held the staff out to Daja. The girl stared at it. What was the design on her staff that had sunk with her ship? Dancing monkeys, each grasping the tail of the one before it, with a wire spiral on her cap, to mark her as a brand new member of the crew. This cap had no mark; it was polished mirror-bright. As *trangshi*, she would never be able to add the signs of her own deeds to it.

Numb, she gripped the wood, and took it from the *mimander*.

"Your name is marked in the books of our people," the

chief judge continued. "You are forbidden to speak, touch, or write to Traders. This is to protect them from you. If you do not wish others to catch your bad luck, do the right thing. Stay away from them."

The woman inked the tip of her brush, and began to write in the book, putting down Daja's new status, for all Traders to know.

"You don't have to do this," Niko protested to the judges. "You have rites to cleanse her luck, rites to make an orphan new-born to a new family, blameless of everything that has gone before."

The *mimander* tucked yellow-gloved hands into wide yellow sleeves. Daja could just barely see eyes behind the thin saffron veil. "We made this choice after taking the omens. I placed sacred oil and my own blood on a hot brass dish, and read the signs for her future. Her fate is to be *trangshi*. There is nothing you can say to change that, Niklaren Goldeye."

"It's all right," Daja whispered to Niko. "They just want to keep my bad luck from ruining anyone else. I understand."

Her rescuer glared at the judges, and tucked Daja's arm in his. "I'm taking her to Winding Circle Temple," he told the Council, his dark eyes sparkling with anger. "*They'll* appreciate her, with or without Trader luck!"

In Sotat:

On their first night outside the walls of Hajra, Niko and Briar slept on the ground at a Trader camp, the welcome guests of a south-bound caravan. On the second night, they stopped at a wayside inn. Briar was inspecting the room that Niko had taken for him – and considering a raid on the kitchen – when Niko called, "Would you come here? I have some shirts I think will fit you."

Unsuspecting, the boy went into Niko's room, to be brought up short by the sight of a large metal tub, filled with hot water. Next to it was a stool with fresh clothes, a scrub-sponge, towels and soap on top. "Hop in," Niko said pleasantly. "The landlady says you don't sleep in one of her beds until you've bathed. I have to admit, I would welcome the change myself."

Briar started to back up. "That stuff's unhealthy," he informed Niko. "Maybe you wouldn't be so bony if you stopped doing *this* all the time."

Strong arms grabbed him: an hostler had been standing behind the half-open door.

"My thinness has nothing to do with bathing," Niko retorted. "Do you undress yourself, or must we do it for you?"

In the end, it took him and three hostlers to give Briar a thorough scrubbing with hot water and soap. The boy's curses, in five different languages, left Niko unmoved, though the hostlers were impressed.

"I never thought a person could *do* all them things," one of them said to another.

"They can't – leastways, not all at once," replied his friend.

Briar was silent all the way downstairs. Only the sight of the loaded supper table thawed him, and that just a bit. "Soon as we're out of Sotat, me'n you part ways," he told Niko. "Even the Street guard only tortures folk when they'd *done* something."

"You'll do as you wish, of course," Niko replied, sitting. "Beef or chicken?"

"Both. And some of that yellow cheese."

"It just seems a pity," the man said, handing over the cheese-plate. From a pocket in his over-robe, he drew out a handful of wilting plants, and put them on the table. "These fell out of your clothes. This" – he tapped a leafy stem topped with a small lilac flower – "I believe is thyme. I don't recognize the others."

Though he pretended not to see the plants he'd stolen over the past two days, Briar reddened. "What's a pity?"

"Magic Circle Temple has the finest gardens – and gardeners – north of the Pebbled Sea. People who know more than I about plants from all over the world." Niko cut a bit of fish for himself, put it in his mouth, and chewed it carefully, without looking at his companion. When he'd swallowed, he added, "It's also one of the two great schools of magic north of the Pebbled Sea. I studied at Lightsbridge, the university for mages, but in some ways I find the mages at Winding Circle more – open-minded."

"Oh, magic, who cares?" Briar dug into his food, refusing to talk any more until it was in his belly, where no one could take it from him. Plants from all over the world? What must that be like?

"I believe there is a dedicate at Winding Circle who has been able to grow vegetables and fruit – even trees – inside a building," Niko remarked. He wasn't even looking at Briar, but at the view from the inn's window, of the seashore.

Briar just couldn't imagine it.

"One thing that I really feel I must say." Niko put greens on the boy's plate. "If I'm forced to bribe hostlers at night to help you bathe, that means less money for food like this as we travel."

Briar glared at him. If Niko saw the dirty look, he chose to ignore it. Instead he returned to eating his dinner.

I'll stick as far as the border, thought the boy. *Get a few more meals like this under my belt – so I guess I'd better do this bath thing. After that, we'll see.* Maybe *I'll have a look at this Winding Circle place; maybe I won't.*

The Pebbled Sea, off Capchen:

Their first night out, the captain invited Tris and Niko to share the evening meal with the officers. The captain himself was delayed, which gave Tris a chance to examine an odd display on the wall near his map-table. It looked to be a collection of knots tied in thick cords, each hanging from a single nail. She counted two in green, one in yellow, one in blue, a fifth that was green with a thin yellow strand in it, and a sixth, green with a blue thread. About to touch them, she changed her mind. They seemed to shimmer, promising a scare to anyone rash enough to handle them.

"There's my treasure, little girl." The captain had come in. "A fortune in winds, that is."

Tris pushed her glasses higher on her nose. "I don't understand."

"It's the work of *mimanders* – Trader mages," he explained. "For a small fortune they'll take a cord and tie a bit of wind up into it for you. See, it's green for north, yella for east, red for south, blue for west, just like they do it in the Living Circle temples. Them's for blowin' us all the way out of any tight spots. And I got one for northwest, and one for northeast. Those'll blow me to safe harbour in Emelan, if ever we need it."

He ushered Tris to her chair. "People can tie up a wind with a knot?" she asked, eyeing him sharply. "You're telling me a tale."

"It's a tale I paid for in gold," the man replied, forking slices of ham on to his plate. "Pass Master Niko the bread, there's a good girl."

She ate quietly, paying little attention to the men's talk. The knots occupied her mind. How could anyone tie up wind in a knotted cord? Was it an easy thing to learn, or hard? She'd never heard of it before – was it a thing only Traders knew?

As the first mate filled their cups, she saw that Niko was watching her. Again, those large, black eyes gave no clue as to what he thought. *Why did the man have to* stare *so?* she wondered. *Didn't his mother teach him it was rude?*

"Why don't you *ask* me anything?" she demanded abruptly. "If you've something on your mind, tell me!"

Niko's eyelids fluttered – was he laughing at her? "I can't," he said, tearing a piece from a sheet of flatbread. "Any questions I have might limit how you think, and the way you act on your thoughts. You see, Tris, just now your mind is unformed, without prejudices. If I present you with the wrong ideas, they might restrict what's inside you."

She thought about that for a few moments, ignoring the smiles of the ship's officers. "That makes no sense whatever," she replied at last. "I'd like an answer that makes sense, if you please."

"Not yet." Scooping up a mouthful of hommous in his bread, he squeezed some drops of lemon on to it. "We have to get to know each other better." He popped the bread and dip into his mouth and chewed.

"That's just his way, youngster," the captain explained, passing a dish of olives to Tris. She muttered her thanks and took some. "Master Niko, he's as hard to understand sometimes as any oracle. When the fit's on him, he can talk you so confused you'll forget which bearing is north."

"It's the university education," Niko told them. "It teaches us to chase our tails for an hour before breakfast, just to get the exercise."

"University?" Tris enquired, interested in spite of herself. "Some of my cousins are at universities. Which one did you go to?"

After a moment's hesitation, Niko answered, "Lightsbridge, in Karang."

Tris shoved an olive around her plate. "My cousin Aymery studies there. He's to be a mage. Maybe you know him? Aymery Chandler?"

"I haven't been there in five years," was the answer. "Chances are that I don't." He poured fresh pomegranate juice for her, then said, "Would you like to be a mage yourself?"

How could he keep taunting her this way, suggesting she could have the one thing she knew she didn't? "No! I *hate* mages! They confuse people!" Jumping up, Tris ran out of the cabin.

Alone on deck, she heard thunder growl in the distance – the storm that had threatened all day was breaking. Darting over to the rail, she turned up her face, just as a tall wave slapped the ship. She was immediately soaked, and her anger washed away. Shaking water from her spectacles, she wondered how it was that she felt queasy in her cabin, but perfectly fine now, with the deck jumping under her feet. It must be the smell, she decided. The cabin smells like all the cargoes these people have ever carried, and maybe some extra.

Here she felt wonderful. Nature roared and thrashed around her, making her rages and tears alike seem meaningless. It was grand to let them go, if only for the time spent out in the weather.

Looking at the choppy seas before her, she noticed dim shadows cast on the white-capped water. Where did the light come from? Even the torches wouldn't burn in this. Turning, she saw nothing at eye level, but something bright drew her attention up the length of the main mast. There, at the top, dim light balanced on the wood. It had to be Runog's Fire, the ghostly flame that seamen believed was the lamp of the water-god, leading Runog either to bless good ships or to sink bad ones.

Shimmering, the light flowed along the topmost yard, until she could see a glowing cross high overhead. A globe of fire leaped to another mast, clinging to its top. Tris laughed gleefully at the wonder before her.

As if it were a living thing drawn to the sound, the light trickled down both masts in glowing streaks, abandoning the upper reaches. Once it was close to the deck, it turned into balls the size of her head, and jumped free. Unthinkingly Tris held out both hands, palm-up, and caught the globes.

Her skin prickled. Each hair on her head rose. Her wool shawl gave off sparks. Then Runog's Fire went out, leaving her to be just plain Tris again, with hair that frizzed even worse now, standing on end. She pawed at it in vain, trying to brush it flat, before anyone came and saw.

A hand thrust a comb in front of her nose. Turning, she glared at Niko. "I suppose you were watching."

"You told me yourself that's what I always do," he reminded her. "And in a sense you are right – I *am* always watching – though not for the reasons that you appear to expect."

"Do you see a monster, like everyone else does?" she demanded, struggling to yank the comb through her bristling hair. "Am I someone who ought to be locked away?"

Coming over, he put a hand on her shoulder. "I see a young girl who has been very badly treated." Try as she might, Tris could hear no pity in his voice. If she had, she might have struck him. "Anything that Winding Circle has to offer will be an improvement on what you've had so far."

She thrust the comb into his hands, and broke out of his light hold. "I need my brush," she informed him, and went below. Inside her cabin, she sank down on the pile of her luggage, trembling. She knew it was stupid to hope that he was right – all her hopes before had been destroyed – but she couldn't help it. Maybe Runog's Fire was a sign that she might be right to hope.

CHAPTER THREE

At Winding Circle Temple, in Emelan:

Sandry toyed with her fork, bored almost to tears. She wished that the servers would serve. If they did, the other well-born maidens at her table would refuse to chatter with full mouths, and her aching ears would get a rest. It wasn't as if they ever said much that was of interest: all they spoke of was fashions and marriages. By now, after nearly eight weeks of their companionship, Sandry was sure that she was interested in neither.

All around her, the dining hall thundered; meals here were booming chaos punctuated by food. When quiet fell, starting near the door and spreading out, it came slowly.

"Oh, no – they let just *anyone* in here, don't they?" Liesa fa Nadlen whispered to a friend. Sandry looked in the direction of Liesa's well-bred glare.

A black girl stood near the door, cup, platter and eating utensils clutched to her chest. In her thigh-length tunic and leggings, both an eye-smarting shade of red, she could only be a Trader. She was big for a young girl, broad-shouldered and thick-waisted. Her skin was the colour of the new, fashionable drink called chocolate; she wore her black hair in a number of short braids. Her lips were locked tight, as if to keep them from trembling.

"Hey, Trader," a boy demanded, "who'd you rob today?"

"Whose baby did you kill to magic wind for your sails?" called someone else.

"Find a seat," ordered the dedicate who ran the dining hall, her voice sharp. "No one can serve until you have a place."

Everywhere people spread their legs, or moved apart on benches, or placed books and packs beside them. They didn't want a despised Trader at their table.

Sandry got to her feet. Liesa's voice cut through her burning anger: "Lady Sandrilene! What are you *doing*?"

She ignored the other girl, and walked briskly across the room. The Trader was glaring at everyone, her chin up, the dark skin of her cheeks burning red. Only when the smaller girl halted before her did she look down.

"My name's Sandry. Please join me at my table." Seeing the other girl blink, guessing that she hadn't understood, Sandry tucked a hand under the newcomer's elbow and tugged her in the right direction.

For a moment, she thought that the Trader might refuse – she didn't budge. Then she relaxed. "All right, *kaq*," she muttered in Tradertalk. "But nobody will thank you for this." She let Sandry pull her between rows of tables.

"If thanks was what I wanted," Sandry replied in the same language, "I would be sad indeed. Since I don't want it, I won't miss it."

The black girl stiffened. Finally she said, "Your accent is *terrible*."

Sandry beamed up at her. "Yes – I know."

"We don't want her with us," protested Liesa when they reached the nobles' table.

Sandry looked down her button nose at the other girl. "She

is my guest," she said flatly. "She— What's your name?" she asked in Tradertalk.

Daja nearly refused. When she saw anger on the faces of the other girls, she grinned instead, white teeth flashing against dark skin. "Daja Kisubo."

"Lady Daja is *my* guest," Sandry told Liesa.

A girl nearby muttered, "If *that's* a lady, *I'm* a cat."

Reaching out, Sandry lifted the pitcher of milk from the table. Cradling it in both hands, she walked over to the mutterer. "I am Sandrilene fa Toren, daughter of Count Mattin fer Toren and his countess, Amiliane fa Landreg. I am the great-niece of his Grace, Duke Vedris of this realm of Emelan, and cousin of her Imperial Highness, Empress Berenene of the Namorn Empire. *You* are Esmelle ei Pragin, daughter of Baron Witten en Pragin and his lady Colledia of House Wheelwright – a merchant house. If I tell you my *friend* is a lady, then *you*" – carefully she poured milk into Esmelle's plate – "*you* had best start lapping, kitty." She set the pitcher down, and returned to her chair.

Daja was still on her feet. "You did no one any good with that," she said in Tradertalk. "Not for me, not for you, not even for them."

"I don't care." Sandry spoke in Common, so that everyone understood. "My papa said that nobility has no right to be rude. We are *supposed* to know better." She plumped her bottom on to her chair, and looked at Daja. "Are you going to sit?" she asked. "Big as you are, you look like you can't afford to skip meals."

For the first time since the sinking of Third Ship Kisubo, Daja smiled. Gingerly, she sat. "I hope other nobles aren't like you." She had a lilt in her speech when she spoke in Common. "I don't think I could stand the excitement."

Novices began to carry bowls and platters to the tables. Any talk about what had just taken place was drowned out in the rattle of wood and metal.

"Trisana, listen to me – I have your best interests at heart." The blue-robed dedicate stood over her, blocking the light. "These odd ways of yours make you no friends with the other girls. They're outside enjoying this splendid weather. You should be, too. If you are to make anything of yourself, you need friendships with girls who will remember you, and help you to meet the right kind of people."

Does she ever shut up? wondered the redhead, as she turned a page in her book.

"Please, give me your attention!" Dedicate Staghorn took the girl by the arm and pulled her up, until she was sitting instead of lying on her cot. "Stop slouching. Put that book down."

Tris attempted to yank out of the woman's hold, without success. She looked up into Staghorn's face with eyes that glinted like grey ice behind her spectacles. "Let go," she said quietly.

"This is for *your* benefit," the dedicate told her. "Whatever caused your parents to give you to the Living Circle temples..."

They didn't want me, so shut up, Tris thought miserably, pale skin crimson with humiliation. *Shut up shut up shut up—*"

Across the room, shutters banged as they closed, then flapped open.

Staghorn jumped, and released the girl's arm. "Now listen. You have been in this dormitory for six weeks, and you act as if you are royalty – you aren't." Staghorn jerked as a door slammed. "You need to be nicer to people."

Tris couldn't answer. Her head was starting to ache, and her stomach lurched unpleasantly. Pressure built in her ears until she thought they might burst. The room pitched before her eyes. This was very different from just being angry. "You wanted me to go out?" she gasped, standing up. "I'm going." Running to the door, she yanked it open. "You might want to come, too!"

The air popped. Staghorn lurched. "If you've made me ill—"

A water pitcher marched off a bedside table, and shattered on the floor. The metal-and-enamel image of Yalina, goddess of water, dropped from the shelf on which it sat. In the corner, a free-standing closet fell over.

Staghorn ran for the door that Tris still held for her. "Quake!" screamed the dedicate. "It's a quake!"

"She noticed," muttered Tris, following her outside.

The ground stilled almost immediately, but Winding Circle's residents stayed outside for a while, in case there were more shakes. Many were fearful: it was the first good-sized tremor in over a year. Was it a warning of a larger quake to come?

Tris yawned. Her sickness gone with the shaking ground, she thought the others' fear was silly. Except for broken crockery and the ruined pine wardrobe, there was little damage – not enough for the fuss that was being made of it, in her opinion. She was also sure there wouldn't be a bigger shake that day, though she couldn't have said how she knew.

Looking around, she saw that Staghorn was huddled with the other two dedicates who supervised the main girls' dormitory, talking rapidly and watching Tris. Straining her ears, the redhead heard: "…knew it was coming."

That was enough; she'd heard people say such things about her dozens of times before. Next would come, "We/I don't want her living here." Book in hand, Tris walked toward the rear of the garden. Out of sight of the dedicates, she climbed over the short fence, and escaped to Winding Circle's biggest library.

In the dormitory, two weeks after her first meal with Sandry, Daja decided to take a late-evening walk, before the dedicates called the girls inside for the night. She walked a great deal these days, feeling trapped inside Winding Circle's twelve-foot-thick walls. She wished she were aboard a sturdy little ship bound southwest, through the Long Strait and the Bight of Fire, into the vast stretch of the Endless Ocean. In recent years word had come of islands in the Endless, filled with strange animals and copper-skinned natives. She would like to see them.

She did *not* like to see her staff, leaning against the wall between bed and nightstand. Its brass cap gleamed like gold, throwing back her distorted reflection. She was sick of it, and of everything it represented.

Leaving it there, she went outside. The sun was below the walls that circled the temple community, leaving shadows to gather inside. She took her bearings: there was the tower the locals called the Hub, dead centre in Winding Circle, pointing to a clear sky.

Daja set out, picking her way through the multitude of small gardens which were fitted between every building inside the walls. Though she was trying to think of other things, she couldn't make herself forget that Winding Circle's smithies were just a short walk away. For a moment, she thought she felt the heat of forge-fires on her skin, and smelled the tang of iron and brass.

It had always been an embarrassment to her family, her interest in metalwork. To be interested in it still, while they slept under the waves, seemed disloyal.

She was trying so hard not to think of the smithies that she didn't know she had company until a hoarse voice growled, "Grab the stinking Trader!"

Daja spun, paying attention now, but too late. Rough arms grabbed her, and dragged her between a gardener's shed and one of the laundries. More hands tried to cover her mouth. She yanked her head away and kicked out with her feet. She hit something hard, and a voice – a boy's, she thought – yelped.

"Kaq!" she snarled, furious as much with herself as with them. How could she have been so careless? "Too *afraid* for a real fight—"

"Shut her up!" someone urged, a girl. She was another resident of the dormitory where Daja slept. "If they hear…"

"Nobody wants you here, Trader!" panted the one who had grabbed her from behind. Daja was flailing, trying to yank herself free. "You stink up our air…"

She kicked something else, something soft. One of them began to vomit.

Light flared, brighter than even sunlight in these shadows: Niko stood in the opening between the buildings and the road, his upraised hand glowing. He had a companion: the assured, worldly black woman who was the Dedicate Superior in charge of Winding Circle, Moonstream.

Daja's attackers – three girls and two boys – ran. She

stumbled and fell when the boy who had been hanging on to her let go.

Hands as dark as her own helped her to her feet. Daja found herself looking into Moonstream's wise brown eyes. "Are you hurt?" the older woman asked. Her voice was clear, low and kind.

"Just my pride," Daja muttered. "I was stupid, and *kaqs* got me."

"I'd hoped our boarders were more open-minded about Traders. I'm disappointed that I was so wrong." Now that she was certain Daja was unhurt, Moonstream's voice was dry and emotionless. She tucked her hands into her sleeves, and looked up at Niko. "Perhaps the girls' dormitory *isn't* the best place for Daja. I'd like her to feel she's safe where she lives."

"Discipline, then?" Niko suggested. "No, it's not punishment," he hastened to assure Daja. "It's the name of a much smaller cottage, near the Earth Temple."

'You'll move there first thing tomorrow," Moonstream said. She laid a cool, dry palm against Daja's cheek. The girl smelled a hint of cinnamon on the dedicate's skin. "Do you think you'll be bothered tonight?"

Daja shook her head. Trouble at night came only as talk. The dedicates who looked after the girls checked the beds too often for any blows to be struck.

"Discipline will suit you better, Daja." Niko put an arm around her shoulders. "You'll have your own room, for one. Privacy can be a blessing in itself."

I'm condemned to spend the rest of my life among kaqs, the girl thought sadly, returning to the dormitory. *There aren't any blessings left for me.*

As she opened the outer door, she heard Moonstream say, "Now – I want to find the ones who did this."

The only problem with lairing under his bed, as Briar discovered on his third night in the boys' dormitory, was that there were no really secure exits. Back home, no one could have sneaked up on him as the other boys did now, blocking him on two sides of the bed as they dragged him out through the third. In Sotat, he would have been down a tunnel and into the mazes of the sewers before they'd blocked his main entrance.

He'd been so busy examining the plants he'd stolen that day that he hadn't heard them coming up. *I'm gonna deserve my ouches*, he thought, grey-green eyes giving no sign of his feelings. *Letting a bunch of dung-footed gawps nab me!*

Two of them lifted him, gripping him by the arms. The fatty loudmouth from three beds down stood in front of him, hand on one hip. He shoved the first finger of the other hand into Briar's face. "*You* stole my cloak-pin, gallows-bait!" he cried. "I want it back!"

Briar knew the pin that was meant; the boy had showed it to everyone the day before. *"Me?"* demanded the street rat, horrified. "Nick that piece of flash? There's no pump worth his Bags as would pay more'n a few copper pennies for it!"

"Liar!" cried his accuser. "It cost me two silver crescents!"

Briar lifted his eyebrows. "Silver-gilt paint, tin and a glass pearl? Then you was nicked, and nicked proper."

Two of the other boys upended the small clothes-chest at the foot of bed, spilling its contents on the floor. Someone else dragged everything out of Briar's den, and scrabbled through the green bits that Briar had just been examining. "Look at this!" he said, laughing. "Did someone tell you dead plants are *valuable*, street scum?"

"*Here's* wickedness." One of the pair searching his

clothes-chest held up two of the knives that Briar had picked up on his journey to Winding Circle.

"Planning to murder us in our sleep, and rob us all?" The leader's finger stabbed forward, poking Briar rudely in the nose.

Quick as a flash, Briar lunged forward, and bit down on the accusing finger. His victim screamed as he hung on. The pair holding him twisted his arms up behind his back. Briar got rid of one, kicking his knee till the boy collapsed. Releasing the leader's finger, Briar smashed the other boy hanging on to him with the back of his skull. His victim fell back, nose bleeding.

Dropping, Briar rolled away from the boys, one hand going to an ankle-sheath, the other going to one in an armpit. Lurching to his feet, he showed them his blades.

"Back up, bleaters, 'less you want more mouth than you got," he snarled.

Softness, like clouds, wrapped around his arms, pinning them to his sides. He couldn't see it, but he *felt* it as it flowed down his legs. When it tightened, it snapped his feet together, knocking him off-balance. He fought it as he dropped, without result.

A foot rolled him over. He quieted, seeing who stood over him: a pair of dedicates. Both wore the yellow habit of the Air temple, which ran the dormitory, but the hem of the woman's robe was lined in black.

"I *knew* what would happen when they let that guttersnipe in!" The male dedicate hauled Briar up by his shirt. "You're out of this dormitory. If I have my way, you're out of Winding Circle altogether."

"What've you done to me?" Briar snarled as the woman tried to pry his knives from his fingers.

She smiled. "Don't like the Shackles of Air, lad?" she asked. "Never saw this kind of magic before?"

Briar went still. *Magic? But that's fakery!* he thought, shocked. Then he looked down at his body. Fakery he couldn't see had glued his legs together and his arms to his sides. When the woman tugged again, he released his knives. The time to fight was over.

"He stole my cloak-pin!" cried his original accuser. "It cost me three silver astrels!" If his friends noticed the change in price, they kept quiet about it.

Briar sighed. "And I told *you*, I won't lower myself. *There's* the bleater that nicked it." He nodded toward the boy who had made fun of his plants. "It's under his pillow."

The boy he'd accused flinched. Two boys went to his bed, and lifted his pillow. There was the stolen pin, as well as a few small treasures belonging to the other boys.

"He put them there!" cried the real thief. "He-he knew we were on his trail, and-and he put them on my bed!"

"Will you swear to that before a truthsayer?" asked the female dedicate. "One of the best is here, visiting Honoured Moonstream. I'd love to see the spells he uses."

The thief swallowed hard, and shook his head.

"Whatever else, I want *him* out of here," the man holding Briar snapped. He shook the boy hard. "Knives have no place in a boys' dormitory!"

"Depends on the dormitory," muttered Briar. The invisible bonds around his legs vanished, and the two dedicates steered him roughly towards the door.

Tris Chandler leaned on the window sill in Winding Circle's administration building, glaring at the clouds. Through the closed door of the Dedicate Superior's office, she heard

Staghorn's whine. The dedicate wanted her out of the girls' dormitory.

Here I go again, Tris thought angrily. *We don't want you – move along.*

Storm-clouds rolled by, heavy with rain and thunder. Lightning danced in them, growing as it skipped from curve to curve, gaining strength with each bounce. She could almost smell its pale, cold scent; the hairs on her arms prickled with its closeness...

Crrracckkk!

The bolt struck ten feet away, crisping a sapling tree. The girl's ears rang; every hair on her head stood upright. In the office, Staghorn shrieked in terror.

Tris smiled.

"Are you all right, Tris?" a familiar male voice asked loudly. "You were looking right at it."

Trying to get her wiry red curls to flatten, Tris ignored Niko.

"It's curious to see lightning hit a small tree where there are tall ones, or buildings, at hand," he added now.

Tris pushed her spectacles higher on her long nose and turned to glare at her former travelling companion. She had to lean back to do it: he was a foot and a half taller than her own four feet four inches. "What have buildings and trees to do with it?" she demanded.

"Lightning strikes what's nearest the clouds," he replied.

"Does it strike the Hub?" she asked, looking at the high tower next door to Administration.

"It has, but the Hub's protected. There's a rod on the clock tower, attached to a wire that runs into the ground. The lightning is drawn to the rod first, and the wire takes it into the soil, where it dies. Except, it seems, on a day like today, when the lightning was invited to strike elsewhere."

"Is that Niko I hear?" Honoured Moonstream opened her door and looked out. Her plum-dark lips smiled a welcome; her brown eyes sparkled. "Come in here – I need you."

Tris turned back to the window.

A hand – warm, solid, almost comforting – rested on her shoulder. Before she could shrug off both it and the comfort, Niko said, "Mages have a very wise rule: before all else, *do no harm.*"

Before she could think of a reply, Niko entered the Dedicate Superior's office, and closed the door.

The outer door banged; two more guests rushed in. One was a pale, sweating dedicate in the blue habit of the Water temple. Tris knew her; she was the woman in charge of Pearl Cup, where the wealthy girls lived. Her companion was Tris's own age. "Sit *there*, away from the window," the dedicate told her charge. "I don't want lightning to hit you until *after* you're not my problem any more – *my lady*. Gods bless us, that was close!" She thrust her companion on to a bench against the wall, then swept into the office without knocking. "Honoured Moonstream, I've had enough!" she cried, and slammed the door.

"Did you see that *lightning*?" The new girl was excited more than scared. "My hair stood on end. I thought *she* was going to take flight!" If the dedicate's words had upset her, it didn't show. "I've *never* been so close to it!"

Tris looked the stranger over. A merchant at heart, like the rest of her family, she knew that the other girl's outfit – a sleeveless black overdress with tightly fitted bodice and jet buttons, a white lawn undergown with puffy sleeves – was costly. Every inch of the newcomer, from the sheer, black veil over light brown braids to the gold embroidery on neat kid slippers, proclaimed old blood, and old money.

Without a word, Tris turned back to the window. This noble would learn her mistake soon enough. She would be ashamed to remember she had spoken to a merchant girl. "It's only lightning," she replied.

The girl came over. "Oh, look, that poor tree got fried." She leaned through the casement eagerly. The band that secured her veil slipped, making the black silk puff on top of her hair.

Tris smiled wryly.

The stranger turned her head. Sky-blue eyes met her grey ones. Instantly the other girl's hand went to her veil. "They *never* stay on straight." She yanked it off. "And no mirror to fix it with. Too bad. I hate veils anyway."

The office door opened. Moonstream walked out, followed by the dedicates who had brought the girls there. "You two are not fitting into the dormitories." The Honoured Dedicate smiled, inviting them to share her amusement. "I am told that, if you were to stay, the other girls will be demoralized. Very well. Today you move to Discipline cottage – it's by the north gate. I think you'll both do better there." She looked at the dedicates. "Pack their things and send them to Discipline. Niko, will you escort Lady Sandrilene and Trisana to their new home?"

The man stepped out of her office. He looked the girls over, smoothing his moustache. "I never thought they would end up at Discipline – I'd thought the school would be enough, once they settled down." He spoke softly, as if he were thinking aloud.

Moonstream sighed. "*Niko...*"

"I tried to settle. Honestly, I did." Sandry's bright eyes were fixed on Niko. "Would I do better at this other place?"

The dedicate in charge of her dormitory sniffed disdainfully.

"I don't *want* to settle in," muttered Tris.

Niko grinned at the Dedicate Superior. "It's my pleasure to take them to Discipline," he said.

CHAPTER FOUR

He led them along the spiral road that gave Winding Circle its name, walking its broad loops instead of cutting across them on the many straight paths available. Sandry talked to him, walking backwards part of the time so she could watch his face. "How long have you been here? I wish you'd told me you were here. It's nice to see you."

Niko smiled. "I'm happy to see you, too. You look well."

Sandry grinned, and nearly tripped on the raised border of the road. Tris caught her, letting go as soon as she regained her balance. "Thank you!" Sandry told her cheerfully. "Sometimes I get so busy talking I forget— Are you all right?"

Tris had stopped in the middle of the road. Red-faced a moment ago, she was now grey-white. "Steady her," Niko said quietly, grabbing one of Tris's arms. Sandry obeyed.

Beneath them, like a giant turning in his sleep, the earth rolled, and went calm. All three of them staggered.

Niko frowned. "Another tremor! That's how many since the spring equinox? Five?"

"Six," growled Tris. Her face went crimson when he looked at her; she yanked away from him and Sandry.

"Do you want to tell me about it?" he asked. "I don't recall you having spells like this on our way here."

"No, I don't want to talk about it," snapped Tris. "I don't

talk to anyone about anything any more!" She wiped her sweaty face on the sleeve of her ugly wool gown.

Sandry noticed that Niko, about to say more to Tris, looked at her and seemed to change his mind. "I hope these tremors aren't a sign of a big quake to come," he said calmly, and urged them forward.

The girls shivered, and drew the gods-circle on their chests, for protection.

Leaving the road before they reached the temple's north entrance, Niko opened a small gate, and led them down a path to a stone cottage. Framed by gardens, the house was neat and clean, the roof well-thatched, the shutters and door painted dark green. On either side of the main building, the whitewashed stone supported additions. One was built of solid wood pierced by windows. The other was a wooden frame with sheer cloth screening its open sides.

"Wonderful!" Sandry peered at that addition, curious. The cloth was thin enough for light to enter, but no insects. "I wonder how it's woven?"

"You may examine it later," Niko said. "Go in. This is Discipline: your new home."

When they entered, a boy with coarse-cut black hair was sniffing dried herbs that hung in bunches near the hearth. Seeing the girls, he skipped back, as if he'd been caught doing something that he shouldn't.

"Good morning, Briar," Niko said. "I've brought you some housemates."

The boy glared at them, his eyes a startling grey-green in his gold-brown face. "Oh, wonderful," he replied. "More *girls*."

"It could be worse." The quiet, lilting voice came from a room to Tris's left. "It could be more *boys*." A tall, black girl dressed in a scarlet coat and leggings emerged, carrying a wooden crate filled with belongings. Her face was round and calm, framed by a double handful of braids. She nodded to Niko, who smiled.

"Daja!" Sandry grinned at her – it was good to see a familiar face. "You live here?"

"Since yesterday," the other girl replied.

"We're being punished, all right," Tris muttered. How could she live with a Trader?

"You have a problem with me, *kaq*?" Daja enquired, black eyes flashing.

"Daja!" cried Sandry, shocked. *Kaq* might be the word that Traders used to mean non-Traders, but it was also a very *rude* word.

A tall woman in the dark green habit of an Earth-dedicate came in through a side door. Like Briar's, her skin was golden brown. She wore her curly black hair cut short, and her smile was genuinely welcoming. "Niko, more desperate criminals for us? They must be cleaning house down at the Hub!"

"Dedicate Lark," said Niko, "I'd like you to meet Sandry and Tris." To the newcomers he added, "Lark and Dedicate Rosethorn are in charge of Discipline."

"Welcome, both of you," Lark said, resting a strong hand on each girl's shoulder. "May you weave happy lives here."

Sandry dipped a curtsey. Tris attempted to do the same, but wobbled, and nearly fell. The boy snorted, and Tris blushed.

"This is Briar." Lark pointed to the boy, who scuffed a bare foot across the wood floor. He was taller than the new girls, dressed in sturdy breeches of plain brown cloth, and a white shirt. Where his sleeves should have been, there were only ragged holes – he'd cut them off. Lark pointed to the Trader. "And Daja."

"We've met," Daja and Sandry chorused, and grinned at each other.

"Here's *my* room," Briar announced flatly, going to an open door on Sandry's right. "I came here first, and I'm keeping it. You kids stay out!" He disappeared inside.

" 'Kids'?" Sandry asked, puzzled. "Why is he talking about goats?"

"Kid is thieves' cant for a child," Lark said. "Now – there's another room on this floor." She glanced at the black girl. "Daja says she prefers what's upstairs. We have another spare room there as well."

"Our own rooms?" Tris asked, startled into speech. "I thought this was a punishment place."

"It's for people who are – ill at ease – with the other students at Winding Circle," Lark replied. "Things go better here if our guests have rooms of their own."

Tris glared at the boy's closed door. "May I see the room upstairs?" she asked, thinking, *I want to be as far from* him *as possible!*

"Come on," Daja said. "I'll show you, merchant girl." Going to the back of the long main room, she climbed a steep and narrow stairway. Tris followed her.

Lark started to set the table near the kitchen hearth. Drifting towards the free downstairs room, Sandry kept an eye on Briar and Niko. The boy grabbed Niko, drawing him closer; Sandry entered the empty room and ducked behind the open door, out of sight.

She could hear Briar's hoarse whisper: "It wasn't me nicked them things, Niko. If they told you I did..."

"I know you didn't," replied the man, just as quietly. "But – knives, Briar?"

"I need—"

"Knives?"

"You don't know what it's—"

"Knives?"

Briar gave up.

"I want them," Niko said flatly.

The boy stuttered, outraged.

"*All* of them," insisted the man.

"But it ain't safe," protested Briar. "What if I have to defend myself?"

"The knives, Briar. If you have them, you also have the temptation to use them. *Now*, if you please."

Slouching, Briar left Niko, and Sandry tugged a braid, thinking about what she'd just heard. At last she shrugged – she didn't think Niko would put her anywhere she would be in danger. That decided, she looked around at her new home.

The room was plain and clean, its walls covered with a coat of whitewash. The bed, night table, stool and wardrobe were all roughly made, but sturdy. The desk was slightly better, as was the chair in front of it. The front window gave her a view of the path to the door, and the spiral road beyond.

Going to the window in her side wall, she looked out. This view was of the inside of the wooden frame addition, the one with cloth screens. Long poles braced shutters against the ceiling, to open the sides of the place. A workroom, it contained a pair of long tables, a big spinning wheel and a smaller one, and a pair of hanging looms. Baskets on the floor held bundles of dyed and undyed wool, as well as spools and balls of spun wool, flax, cotton and silk. Near the back wall stood a large floor loom. On its web hung a shimmering cloth, its design not quite visible to her straining eyes.

Lark weaves, she thought, excited. *She could teach* me *to*...

Her spirits fell. She was Sandrilene fa Toren, an heiress who was kin to royalty in two countries. No one had *ever* let her weave, or handle wool, cotton or flax. Silks she might touch, but even Pirisi had said that she spent more time at needlework than was proper – ladies were supposed to like embroidery only for a few hours, not all of the time. Dedicate Quail at Pearl Cup dormitory had lectured her on the condition of her fingers from near-constant needlework, and sentenced her to three nights of sleeping with hands wrapped in salve and cotton.

Maybe Lark will be different, she thought, with very little hope. Maybe.

Tris stuck her head through the long window of the empty room upstairs. Below, past the solid wood shed at the side of the first storey, was a garden that cupped the back and sides of the house. A figure in a green habit knelt between rows of plants. The girl made a face; she hoped that no one was going to expect her to garden. She hated dirt.

Beyond the garden lay grape vines, which meant bees – another thing to avoid. Beyond that...

Her eyes met the wall that encircled the temple community. Built solidly of grey stone, it rose twenty feet into the air. There were stairs that led to the top – narrow ones, spaced every two hundred yards on the wall. Every four hundred yards, a small and solid tower rose above the upper walkway.

Tris blinked. Someone who climbed to the top of the wall would be inside any storm that passed. The winds would strike purely, coming in from sea or fields, with no streets and buildings to catch them and draw out their strength. A city girl, she had always known that the air she felt, even on rooftops, had its teeth drawn as it passed over encircling walls to pick up all the smells of busy humans, not land, sea or rock.

Looking down, she smiled. The roof of the shed under her window was easy to reach. The ground wouldn't be too far below that.

"You like it?" asked the Trader from the door. "The other's fine for me if you like this one."

"I don't mind." Realizing that she was half-out of the window, Tris pulled herself in. "This seems nice." She flopped on to the bed and lay back to stare at the ceiling.

This is their punishment place, she thought, forgetting Daja was still there. *If I'm kicked out, I have nowhere else to go. No one in Capchen wants me.*

I'd best try to stay out of trouble, then. If I can. If something doesn't happen – except something always does.

And what's Niko doing here again? she wondered. *I thought he was supposed to be running "special errands" this spring – unless he finished them all.* She sighed, her mind still buzzing without let-up.

Daja saw that the redhead was lost in daydreams. *Kaqs*, she thought, returning to her new room. *They only look at you when they want something.*

She ran an affectionate hand over the box – her *suraku* – at the foot of her cot. With the Kisubo mark stamped deep into the leather on all sides, no matter where she put it, she knew she was home. It had served her all the way to Winding Circle, and in the girls' dormitory as well.

Gently Daja rubbed the Kisubo imprint with a finger. *If I*

fail here, where can I go? she thought, not knowing that Tris asked herself the same thing. *I am* trangshi, *without family, without a place.*

Then I must not fail, she told herself, taking a deep breath. *Maybe it won't be so bad. I like Sandry well enough, and she speaks Tradertalk.*

"Hello." Sandry was in the doorway, as if Daja's thoughts had called her. "Is this your new room?"

"What a silly question!" Daja went to the crate she'd carried upstairs, and got out the incense pot, candlesticks and god-images. Taking them to a small table in the corner, she began to arrange them.

"I *am* silly, now and then," Sandry admitted. "My mother said I was, anyway."

"If you know, you can stop it." Carefully Daja placed a candle behind Trader Koma's image.

"Then you've never been silly, or you'd know it just creeps up without any warning."

Startled, Daja looked at the other girl, and saw that her blue eyes were dancing. "Oh, *you*," she said, flapping a hand. "Come in, then. Sit down."

"Thank you." Sandry went to the open window, and sat on the ledge. "Is this house a nice place?"

"I've only been here for a day, but – well, Lark is kind." Daja lit a stick of incense in front of the wooden plaque engraved with her family's names. "You'll like her. Rosethorn, the other Dedicate? She is like – well, they are called porcupines..."

"I've seen them. They're like pigs or woodchucks with backs full of long pins."

"You saw them in a menagerie?"

"No, in Bihan, three years ago. In the forest. My parents..." She stopped, then went on, determinedly cheerful. "They loved to travel."

"So how did you come here, if you were in Bihan?"

"Oh – my great-uncle lives in Summersea." She looked out of the window. "My parents died last autumn, when there was smallpox in Hatar, and he was the closest relative. The rest of my family's in Namorn."

As if she heard it afresh, Daja remembered what Sandry had told those girls just two weeks ago: "*...the great-niece of his Grace, Duke Vedris of this realm of Emelan, and cousin of her Imperial Highness, Empress Berenene of the Namorn Empire.*" If Sandry now spoke of her relatives as if they were just normal people, she must not want it generally known that she was almost royalty. "So that's why you wear all that black," Daja remarked. "Somebody told me once that *ka* – landsmen wear black for mourning."

"So are you, I see." Sandry's wave took in the other girl's clothes.

Daja smoothed her crimson tunic. "I—"

"Traders mourn in *red*?" asked a scornful voice. Briar stood in the doorway, leaning against the jamb. "What kind of barbarian thing is that?"

"Red is for blood," explained Daja. She wasn't offended by his tone. *Kaqs* were ignorant. She couldn't expect one to be as polite as real people. "Even a..." she started to say, and changed her term when she caught Sandry's glare. "Even a mud-roller like you should know that much." In Tradertalk, she told the other girl, "And he *is* a *kaq*."

"I haven't spent my life with my fingers in my ears," Briar remarked in clumsy, but clear, Tradertalk. "And I'm not stupid." Switching back to Common, he added, "Beats me how you people don't break teeth on that gabble."

Daja showed him all of hers in a big, warning grin. "Our teeth are stronger than yours, is why."

Sandry interrupted before the boy could answer. "If we're going to share the same house, shouldn't we try to get along?"

"Don't bother with him," Daja advised. "He's just rude and ignorant."

"Not as ignorant as you thought a moment ago," he teased.

Behind him, Tris announced, "I'm starved. When do we eat?"

"Midday's on the table!" called Lark from below.

Tris bolted for the stairs. Briar raced to catch up, but she beat him to it.

"We'd better watch him," Daja told Sandry, closing the door of her room as they left it. Sandry frowned at her, puzzled. Daja tapped the web between her right thumb and forefinger. "He wears the double X – twice a thief. He'd best stay clear of *my* things."

A dark head appeared in the opening where the stairway pierced the floor – Briar had not gone all the way down. "You think I'm a sluggart, kid? *Everyone* knows Traders curse their boodle, so them that nick it meet a terrible end. I'm smarter'n that."

"Nick?" Sandry asked, stepping on to the ladder. "What's that?"

Briar jumped down, out of her way. "Steal. You nick it, you steal it."

"Wonderful," Tris drawled. She was already downstairs and cutting slices from a loaf of coarse bread. Lark set food on the wooden table, as Niko lifted a pitcher of milk from the cold-box set in the floor. "We'll learn thief-slang."

"At least you'll have *learned* something, 'stead of being

just another bleater all your life," retorted the boy.

Lark smiled at him. "Briar, would you tell Rosethorn it's midday? Keep after her so she won't forget to come in."

He backed up a step. Just eating supper and breakfast with Rosethorn had given him a wary respect for her. "What if she bites me?"

Lark glanced at him with gentle impatience, as if he should have known her reply already. "Bite back."

Reluctantly he went out, into Rosethorn's domain: the garden. The path between rows of unnamed green things was neatly swept. He tiptoed down it, careful not to touch a single leaf. Somehow this garden was different from those he'd seen on the way, different even from the other gardens inside these walls. The plants looked more real, more *there*. Each stood in its own mound of dirt, opening leaves to the sun, like a piece of living magic.

He longed to touch them. Fear made him pause. Rosethorn had said that, if he or Daja so much as *breathed* on a plant, they would spend months suspended by their heels in the well.

He believed her. Rosethorn was very convincing.

She was also nowhere to be seen.

He stopped, listening. Dedicates in Air temple yellow walked by on the spiral road, talking quietly. Somewhere a dog barked; a goat blatted. Under it all lay the buzz of countless bees. The great looms in the buildings across the road were silent for once, the weavers having gone to their own midday meal. He would hear if anyone came around.

To his left, someone had run cords overhead. From them, strings reached to stakes embedded in the ground. Twining plants wrapped thin tendrils around each string. *Slap-*

brained, he thought, peering at them. *What are those vines going to do, run off?*

He looked around again; there was still no sign of Rosethorn. Carefully, gingerly, he stepped into the furrow that lay between two rows of the tied plants, bare feet sinking into freshly-turned, somewhat damp, earth. Wriggling his toes in the dirt, he wanted to sprout roots like threads, roots to drink from the land and return its greeting. A bee, thick-bodied and vividly striped in black and yellow, buzzed around his head, wondering what had kept him inside for so long.

He didn't know how to talk to bees, let alone explain a thing as complicated as Dedicate Rosethorn. Instead he knelt to get a closer look at the captive plants. Touching the delicate leaves with careful hands, he felt their pleasure at being in the sun, watered and digging into rich soil, growing proudly with no insects to munch on their tender parts. The cords helped them to show more of themselves to the light. All of the plants nearly sang with happiness, doing the work they were made to do. They welcomed him, reaching out from their cords to wind instead around his fingers, legs and arms.

"*What the—!*"

Flinching, Briar looked around and up. Rosethorn stood on the path, her green habit streaked with dirt and stains, a basket full of dead plants on one arm. Her dark brown eyes blazed. Every nerve screeched for him to flee the expected beating, but he locked himself in place. Running would mean tearing the plants that had wrapped themselves around him, maybe stumbling and crushing them.

She might see that, and wait to get him away from them before she hit him. That he was in for a beating he took for granted; every other adult that he'd met, except Niko, hit every kid he knew. The cause might be different – drink, rage, the kid was in the way – but the result was always the same. He waited for the cuff or the order to get out of there, *now*!

Neither came. After a moment or two, he risked a look at her.

She frowned still, now more puzzled than angry. Her eyes were on *him*, not her plants. One foot gently tapped the flat earth of the path, as if she were thinking.

She worked barefoot.

Rosethorn's eyes followed his. When she saw her own bare toes, she smiled crookedly.

"Do I send a messenger for *both* of you, now?" Lark called from the back door.

Rosethorn extended a dirty hand to him. "Come on out of there."

"Not if you're going to hit me," he retorted. "I'm no daftie."

She raised her free hand. "Mila strike me if I lie."

His faith in gods was not strong, but Mila was *her* goddess, after all, the one she'd given up a normal life for. Just as he was about to stand, he saw the trick. "You'll hang me in the well."

Rosethorn sighed. That foot tapped again, impatient now. "No, I won't. I water this garden with what's in there – I'm not about to poison it."

This made sense. Carefully Briar tried to rise. The plants tightened their hold on their new friend.

"Stop that, you!" Rosethorn muttered, waving her hand at the vines. "You know better. Behave!"

Tendrils released his arms and ankles, returning to the strings that guided them to the sun. When Briar was free, he stepped on to the path, cringing when the dedicate reached out and gripped his chin in a firm and dirty hold. This close, he saw that she was a hand's length taller than his own five feet of height. About thirty, she had broad shoulders, long legs, and a square, firm jaw. Her auburn hair was trimmed close to her head on the sides, and parted neatly on the left. She'd said little the day before to him or to Daja, except to threaten them with regard to her garden. Now she searched his eyes for something; he wasn't sure what.

At last she let him go, and stalked towards the house. Reaching the well, she drew a bucketful of water. "Come *on*, boy," she called, seeing that he hadn't moved. "Let's wash up."

The large wooden table had been pulled out from the wall. Benches, their legs hinged so they could be folded and stored under the table, were set on its long sides, while stools were placed at both ends. Niko shared a bench with Daja and Sandry. It was clear that Lark and Rosethorn were expected to use the stools. In her eagerness to put the table between her and the Trader, Tris found that she now shared a bench with Briar. He returned her glare with one of his own. They scooted as far apart as they could.

Lark and Rosethorn crossed their wrists, laying their palms flat on their shoulders, and asked the gods to bless their meal. When they were done, the adults began to pass the dishes of food around the table.

"I can't wait till the vegetables start coming in," said Rosethorn with a sigh. "Especially the tomatoes."

"What are those?" Sandry asked.

"Vegetables," Rosethorn said briskly, helping herself to bread and handing the plate to Briar. "Brought from the far side of the Endless Sea." The boy grabbed three slices and shoved the plate toward Tris.

"Rosethorn's the only gardener to grow them successfully on this side of the Endless so far," Niko told Tris and Sandry.

"Dedicate Crane is trying to grow them in his *greenhouse*." Rosethorn made *greenhouse* sound like *midden*. "So far he's failing." She smiled very sweetly.

"What's a greenhouse?" asked Briar. He drizzled olive oil and aromatic vinegar over his bread. It was habit to soften bread first, after he had once lost a baby tooth on a crust. Here, where the bread was soft, oil and vinegar added flavour.

Rosethorn watched him. "A greenhouse is a building made all of glass—"

"All glass?" whispered Daja, brown eyes huge. "But that's *expensive*!"

"And foolish. Crane thinks he can make fruits and vegetables grow out of season in his – and he can," Rosethorn added hurriedly, when Lark glared at her. "They just don't taste like much. And he can't grow tomatoes at all."

Briar looked down so no one could see the interest in his eyes. So Niko had been telling the truth, and they did grow plants inside a building here! He wondered how soon he might be able to slip away to see this marvel for himself.

Lark turned to Niko and asked, "How long are you with us this time?"

"At least through the winter." He sipped a cup of milk. "His Grace the Duke has asked me to look at the harbour lighthouses, and the Temple Council has a few chores for me. I'm to freshen the crystals in the seeing-place, for one. And there's research I need to do in the libraries." Looking at

Tris, he said, "Once I start that, you might like to come along and let me introduce you to the librarians."

Tris looked at her plate. On the trip from Capchen, he had told her about Winding Circle's libraries, famed throughout the countries around the Pebbled Sea and beyond. The offer was *very* tempting. If the librarians knew her, they might steer her to the more interesting books.

"Niko, you are not a dedicate?" Daja asked. "I thought you must be sealed to this temple, since you come here all the time."

Rosethorn cackled. "He's no dedicate – that would mean he'd have to stay in one place. He's a mage – as rootless as a dandelion seed, drifting on the wind."

Briar and Tris stared at the man who had brought them. Sandry and Daja kept their eyes on their food.

"How else can I see everything I wish to see?" he replied. To Briar and Tris he added, "Yes, I'm a mage. Beyond that, I'm a treasure-hunter. I'm here for now, which is all that really matters."

With that, they ate their meal in silence. Despite the fact that he devoured more than anyone else, Briar was the first to finish. He started to get up.

Rosethorn put a hand on his arm. "Down, boy," she told him. "You ask to be excused from the table, remember? And wait until Lark gives permission." That hand pressed down.

For a small woman, she's strong, he thought with admiration. He sat again. "Can I be excused?"

"No. Listen, you four," Rosethorn said, "while you're here, address problems or questions or needs to Lark. She *likes* children, the Green Man alone knows why.

"I don't like children in my garden – not without my say-so, anyway," she added with a glance at Briar. "Play somewhere else. Tell Lark where you go, always. Me, you leave alone. And that workshop on the side of the house, the one that's mostly wood? That's mine, too. Touch anything in there, and you will die the worst death I can invent."

She looked at each of them in turn, then smiled, showing teeth. "I'm glad we had this little talk." Placing her napkin beside her plate, Rosethorn went outside.

For a moment there was silence. Then Lark said, "Her bark is worse than her bite."

"Bet her bite's poisonous," muttered Daja.

"And with the bark you die *slow*," added Tris. They grinned, then remembered that merchants and Traders disliked each other, and turned away.

"Dedicate Lark?" a voice called through the front door. "I have boxes from the girls' dormitories for your boarders."

"One moment," Lark called. "Briar and Daja, as senior guests, will you clean up, please? Once Sandry and Tris are settled, we'll do a schedule of chores, so no one gets stuck with the same tasks all the time."

Niko hastily folded his napkin and got to his feet. "I'll see everyone later," he said, and followed Rosethorn out.

Lark chuckled. "He thinks he'd get snagged for moving duty. He only does what he wants to, our Niko." Rising, she went to the front door.

As Daja started to gather the dishes, Sandry leaned over the table to grab Briar's sleeve, and Tris's. Halted from leaving the table, they stared at her. "Niko brought you *both* here?" asked Sandry.

"So?" demanded Tris, peeling the girl's fingers off her sleeve. "What if he did? It doesn't mean he owns me, or anything." She stomped across the floor, on her way to claim her boxes from the cart.

Sandry turned her blue eyes on Briar. "He brought you?"

He shook her off. "I don't like nosy Bags," he snapped. Grabbing a bucket, he went out to the well.

"Well, if he's a mage, at least I know how he managed to find me in the middle of the Pebbled Sea," remarked Daja in Tradertalk.

"I was – hidden by magic," Sandry replied in the same language. "So he found you, and he found me – and then he brought us here. Why?"

Daja shrugged. "*Mimanders* have their own reasons for everything they do," she replied. "I'm guessing that mages who aren't Traders are the same. Forget it. You'll just give yourself a nosebleed if you think about it too hard."

Sandry touched her small nose, then shook her head, and went to get her belongings.

Her things set up in her new room, Tris hung partway out of her window, trying to see the clouds. The morning storms had passed, but the sky was far from clear. The wind shifted, bringing unfamiliar voices to her ears.

"... know how chancy divination is." It sounded like Niko. "These images are too diffuse. There aren't enough of them. From their scarcity, I'd hazard that they are about a *possible* future event, not one that is probable."

"We should be able to tell!" This voice was not at all familiar. "If we keep trying..."

Tris wiped her forehead on her sleeve. If crazy people heard voices, why did hers make sense? She'd read about madness: voices told the insane that they were gods, or that the neighbours planned to murder them. *Her* voices always had real conversations. And wasn't "divination" a word for telling the future?

"You must do your best." Tris winced. How did Moonstream become one of her mad voices? "Tell me of any change. And let's prepare for a quake. I'll..."

"Um – Tris?"

She gasped, and nearly fell out of the window. Small hands gripped her skirt and hauled her back into the room. Her feet on the floor again, she whirled to glare at the invader: Sandry. "Don't you *knock*?" she demanded, straightening her spectacles.

"I *did* knock," replied the other girl. "And I called. You just didn't hear me."

Tris shook out her dress with trembling hands. "What do you want?"

Sandry hesitated, taking in the other girl's scowl. *In for a copper, in for a gold*, she thought. "This winter, I – went a little crazy. With embroidery, and needlepoint. I have these hangings, more than I'll *ever* need... I thought you might like one." She retrieved a plump, neat roll of cloth from the bed, where she had dropped it, and held it out.

Tris looked at it, then glared. "Is something *wrong* with you?"

"What on earth are you talking about?"

"Just because we all have to live here together doesn't mean you can forget your rank! Look at you, hobnobbing with a Trader, and now me. You can't *do* that! I'm merchant blood, understand? It's in my last name – Chan-d-ler." Tris spoke the word very slowly, as if Sandry were not quite bright. "You're probably an ei or a fa something."

"That doesn't make any difference." Sandry's mouth was set in a mulish line.

"Only a noble would say something so idiotic."

"Here I'm the same as you!"

Tris's laugh was as harsh as a crow's. "You wear slippers at four silver astrels the pair, cotton broadcloth at six silver creses the yard, and – and silk chiffon that's a *gold astrel* the yard, and tell *me* you're the same?" She tugged hard at her own ugly dress. "There is *definitely* something wrong with you. Go away."

"I was trying to be nice." Sandry placed the hanging on the desk. "If you don't want it, then give it to someone else – I don't care." Chin high, she walked out.

Tris slammed the door, and glared at it; she couldn't see a latch that would stop anyone else from barging in. *A nice thing with a* thief *in the house*, she thought. *Not that I have anything worth stealing*.

The roll of cloth sat on her desk, a cream-coloured temptation.

She thinks I'm stupid enough to believe her, thought Tris. *She thinks people never pretended to be my friend before!*

Curious, she spread the hanging out. It showed a six-spoked wheel, with a different, brightly-coloured bird at the end of each spoke. Flat, the hanging was good-sized, two feet by one foot. It was easy to see how the sticks at the centre of the roll would fit to make a frame, and how the cloth would attach to it.

For a long moment Tris stared at it, thinking about how beautiful it was. *Did she say* she *did this work?* the girl wondered. *That can't be right – probably it was servants, only she claims what they did for her own. Nobles do things like that.*

Gently she traced an embroidered toucan's over-large, gaudy beak. She loved birds – they coasted so beautifully on the wind, or mastered the air with darting turns. Looking around, she found a blank space on the wall that needed to be filled. The hanging could go there, where she could see it from the bed.

If she wants it back, I can tell her she gave it, and I'm keeping it, Tris thought fiercely. That *will teach – what did Honoured Moonstream call her? – Lady Sandrilene.*

Daja, carrying her staff, followed Sandry downstairs. No one else was in the main room by that time. "I take it you heard," Sandry remarked with a crooked smile. Plumping herself on the bottom riser, she put her chin on her hands. "Not all nine-fingered girls have hatchets," she said in Tradertalk. "Some of us just tried to have a conversation with a snapping turtle."

"She is right, you know," Daja told her in the same language. "You should keep to your own kind, not try to make friends with Traders and mean girls with red hair."

The other girl sighed. "Not you, too! No, my mind's made up. I'll make friends with whomever I want, so there. I just need more *uvumi*."

"Patience? Why? Why keep trying?" asked Daja, surprised. "Another noble would have smacked her for what she said. Any other noble never would have bothered with *me*, either."

Sandry made a face. "If I lived like that, I never would have had any friends. See, it was my parents – they travelled all the time, instead of keeping their lands and being in attendance at someone's court. The nobles we visited thought maybe children would get funny ideas from me, so they said theirs were always in the country – or in the city – or sick with something."

"So you *had* to make friends with Traders and commoners?" Daja shook her head, whistling silently. "That is *strange*."

"It was *hard*. Commoners and Traders don't exactly fall over themselves to be friends with nobles, if you haven't noticed. I just learned patience, like I said. *Uvumi*." She grinned up at Daja.

The black girl shook her head. "Lark says I can go for a walk. You want to come?"

Sandry rose, smoothing her skirt. "Another time? I have to finish unpacking."

Daja nodded, and headed out of the cottage.

CHAPTER FIVE

Bearing the staff when she went out was still hateful, but after being jumped, Daja knew she had to carry it, just as any Trader did in an unfriendly town. She planted it solidly in the dirt as she walked, throwing a coat of dust over the new brass and ebony.

It was a beautiful late spring day – growing weather, if one cared for such things. Rows of vegetables, fruits and herbs flourished in the gardens beside the spiral road, a promise of winter food. Channels of water ran between them, so the land drank its fill. Dedicates in Earth-green, like Rosethorn and Lark, and novices in white tended the plants. Other dedicates in Water-blue looked after the irrigation system, making sure that all areas got the right amount of liquid. Passing the western temple, Daja stopped to bow, hands together in front of her face, in respect to the gods of Water.

On the far side of that building, plants were replaced by carpenters' shops. Beyond those were the smithies that lay around the southern temple, which was dedicated to the Fire gods. Today she ignored the soft voice of her upbringing, the one that sneered at her interest in *lugsha* craftsmen in Tradertalk. She watched a sweating female apprentice pour molten copper into a mould, and a master silversmith put the last touches on an urn.

At last her feet drew her to a small, isolated shop tucked

into the shadow of the southern wall. Inside, a black man laboured, his back uncovered and rolling with sweat. Bald on top, he'd let the rest of his hair – as well as his beard – grow long and wild; they swayed as he pounded hot metal. Under a leather apron, the top of his red habit hung from its rope belt, gathering soot as it brushed the anvil.

"Kirel!" he called over the chime of hammer-blows. "I need the top full— Hakoi bless me, I sent him out." Glancing around, he saw Daja. "Girl, a favour? I need my top fuller." He pointed to a long counter, where a number of metal and wood tools waited.

She leaned her staff on the wall and went to the counter. "What's a top fuller?"

"Like a hammer, but the head's rounded..."

For a moment she saw nothing *but* hammers. Then she found one like that looked like his description. "This?" she asked, picking it up. It had weight in her hands, and authority. Her skin prickled with excitement. She'd never touched a smith's tools before.

"That's it!" She thrust the fuller into his grasp. He struck the hot metal with the rounded end, flattening red-hot iron to one side. " 'Prentice – had to – get a bucket," he explained between blows. "Should be back by now."

"What are you making?" she asked, watching the pattern of his strikes. He pushed the metal with the top fuller's rounded head until it bulged like pie crust under a rolling pin. The metal glowed a dull, sullen red, its smell sharp and bitter.

He lifted the piece. "A strap for a door, when I'm done with it."

Daja raised her eyebrows. The metal was already three feet long. "It must be a dreadful big door."

The smith grinned. Not once did the steady blows of his fuller lose rhythm. "It is – the Duke's treasury," he explained. "There'll be eight all told – two of the finished ones are over there." He nodded toward the counter. Next to it she saw a pair of long, thin pieces of black iron leaning against the wall. "Take a look, if you like."

Daja obeyed. The finished strips were four feet long. Something under the surface of the metal moved as she looked at it, like the muscles that flexed under the man's skin. Were there letters in the iron? Frowning, she reached out, then yanked her hand back.

"You can touch them," called the smith. "They won't bite."

Daja smiled, and ran her fingers over the beaten metal. The iron was cold, but warmed quickly when she rested her hand on it. "I thought I saw letters here for a moment," she commented, as much to herself as to the man.

"Letters, is it?" It was hard to tell what he thought from his breathless voice. "Well, you're right. Not everyone sees them, I have to tell you."

"I can't see them – not any more." She rubbed her fingers over the metal. The sound of feet approaching at a run made her flinch, and grab her staff.

"Frostpine, you wouldn't believe how slow they were!" A huge young man with braided fair hair and blue eyes came into the forge, a bucket in each hand. His run had tossed both hair and a soot-streaked white habit out of order. "If I was the duke's grace himself, they still would have taken for ever!" He looked at Daja as he set his burdens down. "So I made them give me *two* buckets."

"Don't fret," the smith replied, thrusting the metal that he worked back into the forge-fire. "This lady helped me."

Going to the water-barrel, he lifted out a dipper full of liquid, and drank it all. The second dipper he poured over his head; the third went down his throat. "What's your name, youngster?" he enquired.

"Daja."

"Well, Daja, would you mind standing by to mop my fevered brow? Then my friend here can put three more bars in the forge to heat, and check our coal supply..."

"Hakoi scorch me, the coal!" cried the youth, and ran outside.

His master winked at Daja. "You may have gathered that I'm Frostpine. That was Kirel, my apprentice."

She ducked her head to hide the grin until, peering at him, she saw that he grinned, too. She took the handkerchief that he offered her. Frostpine shook the water from his hair and beard, much as a dog might, then took a cherry-red piece of metal from the fire.

Tris was half-drowsing on her bed when someone banged on her door and opened it. With a shriek, she sat up. "How *dare*—" Her throat seized on the rest. It wasn't the thief-boy, as she expected, but Niko.

"Come on. Let's take a walk. It's time to sort a few things out."

She scowled at him. "I don't want to."

"*Now*, Trisana."

There was a hint of steel in that clipped voice, and more than a hint of it in the man's black eyes. Dare she refuse? Travelling with him, she had to obey, but now? He wasn't temple. He was a guest, but could she ignore the fact that he was a guest who worked for the temple, and spoke comfortably with Honoured Moonstream?

"Did you ask Lark? Maybe she wants me to learn the house rules..."

"Lark has already given permission. *Up*, young lady."

Grumpily she descended the stairs behind him. She was not beaten yet, however. Seeing Lark in the weaving-room, she put her head in and said, "Lark, Niko wants to take me somewhere."

Lark was sorting through skeins of coloured thread. "That's right, Tris. Obey Niko as you would Rosethorn or me," she replied, her mind plainly somewhere else.

Niko grinned at Tris wickedly. "A nice try. Come on."

Once on the spiral road, he walked so quickly that his grey over-robe flapped behind him while Tris struggled to keep up. They left the temple city through the south gate. Crossing the flat expanse of road that lay between the wall and the cliff, they reached the grass fringe on the far side. When Niko stepped off the cliff's rim, Tris squeaked.

He looked back at her. "There's a path," he told her, amused. "Come on."

Gingerly, she obeyed. There *was* a track of sorts, twisting down through tumbled rock, earth and stunted trees. She scrambled along, catching her skirt on roots. The man stopped on a broad ledge just two hundred yards above the rocky shore. A cave opened on to it, stretching back into the cliff. Tris couldn't see the cavern's rear wall.

"This will do." Niko sat cross-legged just inside the cave's mouth. He patted the ground next to him. "Have a seat."

She mopped her sweaty face on her sleeve. "Why?"

"Because I ask. Because you don't have anything else to do just now. I'd actually meant to talk to you when we travelled together, but – I forget what distracted me."

"You found out the captain had been to the Strait of

Dragons," she said patiently. "You wanted them to tell you about it." She'd enjoyed those tales herself. "And right after I got here, you had to leave again, in a great hurry."

"That's right – I had the vision that Third Ship Kisubo was about to put to sea. Well, nothing's going to interrupt now. Sit, please."

Grudgingly, she obeyed.

He looked at her, and sighed. "I wish that by now you could trust me."

She looked out through the cave entrance, at the clouds. "Everyone I ever trusted sent me away," she said flatly.

For a while he said nothing. Tris, glancing at him, saw a look of pity that made her blush with embarrassment. At last he reached over, squeezed her fingers, and let her go. "Then I will just have to hope that you change your mind someday. In the meantime, you're going to learn meditation."

"Why?" she demanded. "The others don't have to."

"They start tomorrow. As for you, why now?" His eyes held hers; she tried to look away, and couldn't. "Things happen when you get angry, Tris. First hail, now lightning – if you don't learn to control yourself, you will kill someone."

She felt like there wasn't enough air to breathe. Was he saying she was possessed by a spirit, or not entirely human, as they'd thought back in Capchen? There were people who attracted spirits they couldn't control – every child knew those stories. She didn't want to spend the rest of her life in a cage. "How do you know?"

"Do you know we mages choose the name we bear, once we are trained?"

She shook her head.

"We do. My last name is 'Goldeye'. It means that I see things that are hidden to most people. *That's* how I know.

And I tell you this. If you learn to meditate – if you learn to control your mind – you will be able to keep things from happening when you are upset."

She tore her glance away from his and clenched her hands. A chance to stop people blaming her for what she couldn't help? "What do I do?" she croaked.

"Can you breathe with the sound of the waves? Breathe in as they arrive, hold the breath as they strike, breathe out as they go?"

She listened to the sea boom as it struck the rocks below. She drew a long breath; hearing the ocean always had a relaxing effect on her. When the next wave hit, she let her breath run out, following the water as it fell back. Her wind caught in her chest. She cleared her throat.

"Relax," Niko whispered, his voice part of the next wave. It caught her up, lifting her as it struck the shore, then ran out as the sea retreated. Her mind slipped easily under a new swell of water. When it came in, she came with it, breathing in slowly, filling every nook and cranny of her lungs with new air.

"Waves are the voice of tides. Tides are life," murmured Niko. "They bring new food for shore creatures, and take ships out to sea. They are the ocean's pulse, and our own heartbeat."

Tris's eyelids fluttered; her mind rode with the new wave. It struck the rocks with a crash, covering barnacles and mussels. She held her breath for the impact, then let it sigh out with the sea as the water fell away.

"They carry the winds," whispered Niko.

She rose to the back of a new wave as the breeze combed her hair and filled her nose with the sea's tangy odour. When the wave shattered against the rocks, she raced on with the air, rolling up the cliff-side to flow over the top of the bluff and the road. Ploughing head-on into the wall at Winding Circle, she ran up that.

"Breathe out," Niko told her.

Tris was locked on the wind's rush, that was so vivid in her mind. Her body heard Niko, and released the air that it clung to. Her lungs filled again, as the wind/Tris leaped into the sky over the temple city. Here she was buffeted by new kinds of air. It rose from the gardens, rippled over forges and ovens, puffed in the beat of looms, stuttered over the surface of wet clay.

"Feel how you are right now? Like a wind yourself, your wings passing over the circle of the wall?" Niko's voice filtered through her thoughts. "Pull your wings in on yourself. Instead of being a wave of air, draw yourself in until you're a rope of it. Breathe in, and pull in."

It was like gathering the sides of her cape when they were flung out, and wrapping them in around her. When she breathed out, she gathered more folds of herself under the outstretched fingers of her mind, and pulled them in. She shrank into a rope, feeling pressures from the temple's warm spots under her narrow length.

Opening her real eyes, Tris yelped: Niko shone with a blinding white radiance that left dark spots on her vision, as if she'd stared at the sun. Her cry pulled in too much air, and her lungs protested. For a brief moment she felt her mind fling itself out wide again. Then her sense of being anything but Tris was gone.

Niko patted her on the back while she coughed long and hard. As she got herself under control, he offered her a drink from the canteen that swung at his waist. "There, now, wasn't that fun?" he asked. "We'll keep practising that, until you limit the area that your mind covers *without* having to think about it."

He has a strange *idea of fun*, Tris thought, and drank greedily.

When Lark asked him if he would mind taking a note to Dedicate Gorse at the kitchens of the Hub, Briar was happy to oblige her. It gave him the chance to cross the gardens that lay between most buildings on his way, to look at what grew there and breathe in scents. It was also a chance to visit the kitchens and see a dedicate famous for giving treats to visitors.

The way led down a gentle slope. At the centre of the shallow bowl that held Winding Circle, the tower of the Hub rose like the stem of a top. Briar stopped to inspect it, as he'd done on his arrival some days ago, wondering if it would be worth the trouble to burgle it. As always, he decided against it. What he told himself was that too many people worked in the Hub day and night. It was true, and helped him to keep denying that he was done with the nicking life.

It was true that someone was always in the tower. Below the giant clock at its crown were rooms where magic was worked, or so Niko had said. He took that as he did all of Niko's mentions of magic, with a shrug. For Briar, the real magic of the Hub was in the bottom two floors, where enchanting smells flowed through open kitchen windows.

Reaching the tower, Briar inhaled the mingled odours of stew, bread, spices and charcoal. Then, mouth watering, he carried Lark's note inside.

When he left, two pastries stuffed with honey and nuts rested in his belly, and he carried a string bag with another twelve pastries, for Discipline. Now, for a little while, his time was his own.

"Where is the greenhouse?" he asked a novice who laboured in a small rose garden. The girl pointed to the path that ran arrow-straight from the Hub to the east gate. Whistling, Briar took it, and walked right into a shaft of light that nearly blinded him. Blinking, he shielded his eyes to find its source. There, behind the main dormitories for boys and men, stood a clear building over a storey in height.

Pulse hammering, he trotted up to it. As Rosethorn had said, it was real glass, held up by wooden beams. Inside, the air steamed; water condensed on the inner walls and ran in drops like rain, blurring the images of plants, bushes and trees that grew there.

How did it work? Where did the water come from? Could this Crane fellow really grow fruit and vegetables out of season in there? Awed, he walked down one side of the building, staring through the wall. Dedicates in yellow habits tended the plants, so fixed on their work that they did not see the boy staring in at them. Briar wished, more than anything, he could enter. He could pretend to be lost...

As he rounded the corner, stepping into the gap between the greenhouse and a stable that stood against the east wall, something pulled at his heart. He moistened his lips. Suddenly they were dry to the point of cracking. He felt brittle, and squeezed.

Frowning, he placed a hand flat on the glass. There, to the right – the sadness came from that direction. Carefully he walked along, keeping his fingers on the glass. When his palm itched, he stopped. On the other side of the glass stood a tree little more than a foot high. But for its size, it looked like one of the low, spread-branched pines that grew on cliffs along the coast. He squinted, trying to get a better look through misted glass. Some of its twigs were brown.

"Here – what are you doing?" The speaker was a tall, lean man with lank, black hair and a thin, suspicious face. He wore the yellow habit of the Air temple with a black stripe on the hem, the same garment worn by the woman who'd wrapped Briar up in his old dormitory. The lean dedicate's companions, a man and a woman, wore plain yellow, without the stripe. "Boys aren't permitted back here." He sounded bored, but his brown eyes were alert.

Briar glanced at the stable. "But horses are?"

The woman growled. "Mind your tongue, boy! This is Dedicate Crane, first Dedicate of the Air temple, that you're speaking to!"

Crane raised a hand to silence her. "Where are you housed?" he asked, looking down a very long nose at Briar. "Have you permission to creep around?"

The boy offered the iron token that Lark had given him, to show that he was allowed to wander. Crane shoved it under the woman's nose. "Look – it's from Discipline. Rosethorn!" He no longer seemed bored. "Are you her spy, boy? Out to steal cuttings for that patch of scrub she calls a garden? And where did you get those pastries?"

Briar could see that Dedicate Crane was determined to think the worst. Snatching the token from the man's fingers, he ran, leaving the greenhouse, and the sad tree, behind.

Soon after Lark had gone on an errand to the loomhouses, Sandry gave in to temptation and went into the dedicate's workroom. Poking around, she found baskets of fleece that had yet to be combed and prepared for spinning. Sandry knelt beside them, and lifted out a hank of wool. When she touched it, strands rose on end. Wool fibre and thread always moved when she was near; she had no idea why. It certainly didn't follow anyone else that she saw handling it.

"That's Merino wool," Lark said.

Sandry yelped. The wool twisted in her hands, and trapped her fingers.

Lark knelt beside her. "It's my favourite, but I don't use it to teach someone just learning to spin. The fibres are very short, which makes it hard to work with."

Sandry tried to scrape the suddenly contrary wisps off her hand, but they refused to come away.

"It normally isn't disobedient – it must like you. Enough," Lark ordered; Sandry didn't think that Lark meant her. "Let go." She dragged her fingers across the girl's palms. The wool followed her, shaping itself into a neat strip.

"It's a kind of magic," Lark murmured. "Look how fine each hair is. Pick one out – just one." She offered the strip to Sandry. Carefully the girl grasped a single hair and drew it away from the others. "Now pull it apart."

Sandry obeyed. With just a quick tug, the hair snapped.

"By itself, it's weak. There's little work you can do with it." Lark smiled. "Put it back with its friends, and things change."

Sandry reached over and pulled away a few more hairs.

"Roll them together," Lark said. "Twist them, as you would yarn. Now try to pull them apart."

Sandry obeyed. The twisted thread held, no matter how hard she tugged its ends. "I wish I could spin. I wish I could make things stronger. Instead I'm always told nobles don't spin, or weave," she whispered. "They say needlework is all I should want to do, and then they tell me I do too much of *that*."

"Why were you taken before Honoured Moonstream?" the woman enquired gently. "Why were you sent here?"

Sandry blushed, and looked down. "I kept sneaking off to the loomhouses."

Lark drew a bobbin from the pocket of her habit, and pulled an end of thread free. When she let it go, the thread stretched, snake-like, toward her, then to Sandry. When Lark held the bobbin out to the girl, the thread fought to work itself free of its anchor. It twined around Sandry's fingers when she reached for the bobbin.

"Silk likes you, too," Lark said. "That's unusual. Silk likes few people."

Half-hypnotized by the thread's movement, the girl said, "I was – in a dark place, once. My lamps were going out, but I had all this silk embroidery thread." Part of her was shocked to hear the story come out – she had told it to no one, not even to Niko, during their long journey to Summersea. "I thought that I'd called light into the silk." She sighed. "It was probably just a dream, though."

Lark wrapped her brown hands around the girl's white ones. "Do you want to learn how to spin?"

"I would *love* to," replied Sandry.

"Do you know how to prepare wool for it?" Lark asked.

Sandry nodded. "Pirisi, my – nurse – taught me how, when I was little. She hasn't – hadn't – let me do it for a long time. She said I was getting to be a lady."

Gently Larked smoothed Sandry's hair. "Then find me a basket of rolags, if you please, and a drop spindle. One with no leader on it, or thread."

Next to the uncombed wool was a straw basket with a cloth lining; it was filled with the long rolls of combed wool called rolags. Sandry picked it up and offered it to Lark, then found a spindle that had no yarn or thread on it. Bare, it looked like a child's top with much too long a stem.

When Sandry took it to Lark, the woman asked, "Do you know the names of the parts?"

The girl shook her head. "All the ones I ever saw were being used, and I got scolded for asking."

"You won't be scolded for asking questions here." Lark pulled the wooden disk off the stem. "This is the whorl." In her other hand she held up the stick. "Here's the shaft. The whorl fits on the short end like this." She thrust the pointed end of the shaft through the hole in the whorl. Putting the complete spindle on the floor, she gripped the long stem and twirled it, as if she played with a top. Like the toy, the spindle whirled on its point. "With spinning, you learn how to control the spindle and how to feed your wool to it at a steady rate. That's why you see even five-year-old children spinning; it's easy enough, once you learn how.

"I'll show you how to place the leader yarn and how to store your spun thread later. Right now, there's something I need to see." She drew a piece of yarn from a pocket. In a series of quick movements, Lark fixed it around whorl and shaft, and tied it in place. "This string is your leader, the thing which makes the thread happen." She held out a hand. "Give me a rolag."

Sandry took one of the specially prepared bunches of wool from a basket, and put it in Lark's outstretched palm.

"Watch," Lark ordered. Overlapping the end of the wool with the end of the leader yarn, she gave the spindle a gentle twirl. As it turned, Sandry could see the yarn, and the fibres attached to it, twirl until the loose fibres wound themselves into a tight string. Her grip on leader and wool just tight enough to keep everything from slipping from her fingers,

Lark allowed the spindle to slowly drop to the floor, hanging from the new thread. A bit at a time, she let new fibres from the rolag get caught in the twirling thread, until they were thread as well.

"I love this work," Lark murmured. "It's soothing."

Sandry nodded, eyes never leaving the spindle. "No matter where we travelled, I watched the local women as they spun. It always seemed like magic."

"It *is* magic. And there's magic you can do with it, if you have the power. To take something tangled, and faulty, and spin it, until it's smooth and strong – now there's work that's worth doing!" She halted the spindle, keeping her new thread stretched between it and her hand. "Take it. Don't let it spin backward, or the work comes undone."

Nervous and eager, Sandry obeyed. Both spindle and thread felt very warm to the touch. Lark slipped the wool rolag into the girl's right hand, pressing the point where fibre became thread between Sandry's thumb and two fingers.

The girl squeaked with surprise, and dropped the spindle. It whirled in reverse. The leader yarn lost its grip on the new thread, which untwisted itself. She was left with a handful of unspun wool. "Donkey dung!" Sandry blushed. "I'm sorry; I didn't mean to…"

Lark chuckled. "I know *exactly* how you feel. It happens so much *faster* when it all goes to pieces. Pick it up. Lay two inches of leader yarn over two inches of wool fibre." As Sandry obeyed, Lark went on, "Think of something outside the work – your heartbeat, perhaps, or your breathing. Twirl the stem clockwise. Draw the wool gently from the rolag into your thread. Let the spindle drop slowly to the ground as your new thread lengthens."

Sandry trembled still as she flicked the stem to the right.

The spindle twirled. She had to let the tool fall, but she also had to feed bits of wool into the thread. She could only use one hand to steady her new thread, because didn't she have to give the stem of the spindle another twirl? It must be winding down.

She looked down just as the spindle slowed almost to a halt – then twirled in the opposite direction. The thread fell apart, dabs of wool dropping to the floor. "Cat dirt, cat dirt, cat dirt," she muttered, smacking her forehead.

Patiently, Lark helped her to begin again. "Think of a rhythmic sound – one you like to hear. One that's soothing." Lark's voice was soft, and as warm as honey. Listening made Sandry a bit drowsy. "Close your eyes for a moment, and listen for it. I'll help you keep control over the spin."

Eyes shut tight, Sandry listened, though she wasn't entirely sure what she listened for. A rhythmic sound, a soothing one? Her thoughts skipped to the past, to last winter. After she had come out of her cellar, Niko had found her a bedchamber in the Hataran king's palace, above the room where the royal weavers did their work. Lying in bed, staring at the ceiling, at first she had refused to take an interest in anything. Why did she have to? Her entire world was dead.

The beat of looms under the floor pressed on her, though. Without her wanting it, the bump-thwack they sounded, dawn to dusk, wove into her breath and heartbeat. One Sunsday, soon after Midwinter, all the looms fell silent. This happened every Sunsday, which was a rest day, but she had never cared before. Now she was restless, angry. She slept badly. The next day the chorus of looms began at dawn, and she sat up to listen. When Niko arrived an hour later, she still sat up.

Looms sounding in her ears, Sandrilene fa Toren spun.

"I have to wind the thread," Lark murmured. The girl blinked, and looked at her work. With the dedicate to guide her hands, she had managed to spin two entire feet of thread. It was perfect, except that there were four large bumps, each the same distance from its fellows.

"Where did those come from?" she asked, confused. "I didn't feel any lumps."

"You were thinking of new life," Lark replied. "You thought of it, and you spun it."

"Then new life has lumps in it," Sandry remarked. "Let me try this again."

"Better yet, we start afresh. Let's take the old thread off." The dedicate's slender fingers undid the ties that bound Sandry's thread to the spindle. She wound it on to a bobbin, and put it in the girl's lap. "Keep that," she said. "And keep it safe. It's your first thread – it's important."

There was plenty of light remaining in the day when the Discipline residents gathered for supper, without Niko. Carving the chicken, Rosethorn looked around the table and said, "You, boy..."

"Briar," he said quietly. He was afraid to look at her. She might remember that he'd touched the plants that wound around strings, and punish him.

"Briar, you have hands attached somewhere, do you not? Pass the bread to..." Rosethorn squinted at Tris.

"Tris," Lark said helpfully.

Rosethorn made a face. "And you, Sandry – I'll take that." The girl handed over a bowl of rice, lentils and onions.

"And *this* one..." Rosethorn nodded toward the Trader.

Daja stared into space, hearing the ring of fuller on hot metal – she didn't notice that Rosethorn was trying to pass a dish of chicken to her. At last the dedicate thrust it under her nose. Daja came to herself with a start. "What?" she asked, startled.

Briar snickered.

"Daja, is it? I remember now. Well, Daja, would you be so kind as to relieve me of this?" Rosethorn demanded. "Before my hand falls off?"

A blush stained Daja's cheeks. Hastily she took the plate of carved meat.

Rosethorn looked at Briar, who was eating as fast as he could. "Slow down," she ordered. "By the time it reaches us, the food no longer tries to run off the dishes."

Briar met her gaze. Under fine brows – knit together in her normal, irritated expression – she had large, brown eyes with a touch of humour in their depths. His pace slowed. As if his mouth had a mind of its own, Briar heard it ask, "What does it mean when a tree has some green leaves and some brown?" He cringed, waiting for a slap.

Rosethorn frowned. "Did you see it in the autumn?"

"No. Today." She wasn't going to hit him? It's what any grown-up would have done, back in Deadman's District in Hajra.

"Then the stem that has brown leaves is dead. The whole tree may be sick, or dying. Where did you see it?"

He winced. It had been hard enough just to ask. He wasn't at all ready to mention Dedicate Crane. "Around," he said vaguely.

Rosethorn sipped her juice. "Well, if you see it again, *around*, let me know. Perhaps I can help. There's no reason for any Winding Circle tree to be sickly."

Once the table was cleared, Lark took the large slate on the wall nearest the hearth off its hooks and laid it on the table, along with a stick of chalk. "The schedule," she said, black eyes impish. "Yours includes chores and lessons—"

All four of them groaned.

"I *knew* you'd be happy," Lark commented. "Now, first in the day, everyone cleans her – or his – room. Some mess is all right, but make your beds, sweep your floors, and clean your wash-basins before you come to breakfast. After that, we'll do chores inside the house..." She bent her curly head over the slate and began to write.

Briar frowned. "What if I don't know how to do any chore stuff?"

Lark smiled. "We'll show you."

"I've done housework for ever," Tris said glumly. "It's not hard to learn." She looked at the others, wondering how good they would be. Sandry had probably had servants all her life. The only things Tris knew about Traders were tales of secret rituals and how they cheated merchants. Did the tales mention cleaning and sewing? She couldn't remember if they did. "I'd better not get stuck doing all the work," she muttered.

"You won't," Lark replied. "That's why I do a schedule. As the moon goes from full to full, you all share the chores. No one gets stuck with the hardest ones every time."

"We have terrible ways to ensure no one cheats," Rosethorn said, leaning back in her chair. Four pairs of eyes fixed on her as they tried to guess if she was joking or not. The tiny smile on her lips was not at all reassuring.

"After chores," Lark announced, "you learn to meditate, under Niko's supervision."

"What's meditation?" asked Daja.

"It's clearing your mind," replied Lark.

"It's controlling your mind," Rosethorn said at the same time.

Lark smiled. "As you can see, it serves more than one purpose."

"It's priest stuff," grumbled Briar. "Real people don't need it."

"But you're no longer a real person, boy," Rosethorn commented wickedly. "You live here – you're halfway to being a priest yourself."

"Meditation teaches self-control," Lark told the children firmly, with a look at Rosethorn that said *Behave!* "It teaches discipline. You learn to govern and organize your mind. Since a few of you were sent here because you were thought to be ungovernable" – Sandry, Tris and Briar turned red – "meditation could turn out to be the most important thing you do here."

"It can't hurt, and it might help," added Rosethorn.

Lark examined the slate. "After that, midday and clean-up. Then, during the summer, Winding Circle has a two hour rest period, during the hottest part of the day. That time's yours. After it, we'll arrange for lessons of some kind – I'll take care of that sometime this week. Then supper, and clean-up. Here we bathe daily, after supper, in the Earth temple. Free time for a while, then bed." She looked at Daja and Briar. "We didn't take you to the baths last night because you were still getting settled. That was an exception, not the rule."

"Aren't temple baths just for dedicates and novices?" asked Sandry.

"We have permission to bring our charges," Lark replied. "It's easier on everyone." She looked at the children's faces. "Don't look so glum. On Sunsday your time is your own, provided you behave. And there are holidays, and days when your teachers won't be available. We'll try not to work you to death. Any questions?"

No one said a word.

"Then get your bathing things, and meet us here."

The group split up to collect soap and sponges, the undyed robes given to them by the temple, and wooden shoes to keep their feet out of the dirt. When they assembled at the back door, the only one missing was Briar.

Rosethorn stuck her head into his room. The boy was inspecting one of the plants that she had pulled from the ground during the day. "Come on, my lad," she ordered. "That nettle had better go back in the compost heap, where it will do me some good. I don't want it seeding in my garden."

"I washed day before yesterday," he retorted. "How can a plant do good in a heap, and not the garden?"

"It helps the compost to ferment, so the compost makes better fertilizer. The fertilizer helps plants I *want* to grow. If the nettle stays in the ground, it chokes out other plants. Get moving."

He stared at her, grey-green eyes stubborn. "You and Niko! I never washed so much before. I'll catch my death."

"Nonsense. Think how much nicer you smell." When he didn't move, Rosethorn's eyebrows twitched together. "I have used up my week's allowance of patience, boy. *Everyone* bathes here, *every* day. You *don't* have a choice."

He bit his lip. If he refused, she might get rid of him – and she knew about plants. Then he thought of something, and grinned. Unlike Sotat, here the sexes bathed separately. He'd wait until the women entered their side of the bathhouse, and return to the cottage. Making a note to wet his hair to convince them, he gathered his things and followed the others outside.

A slender, long-haired figure in an undyed robe awaited them at the bathhouse. "I hoped to find you here," said Niko with a charming smile. "I thought I'd be company for Briar." He draped a thin arm around the boy's shoulders, steering him toward the door to the men's baths. "I know all these new experiences must be unsettling for you."

Briar scowled at Lark and Rosethorn, who ducked their heads to hide grins.

"Have a nice wash," Sandry teased as she walked by.

"Make sure to get behind your ears – *kid*," Daja added.

"Where did she learn that bit of street argot?" enquired Niko. "No, don't tell me – I know. Come, Briar. The sooner we begin, the sooner you can dry off."

As the girls entered the main chamber of the women's baths, Tris backed up a step, shaking her head. "*Now* what?" demanded Rosethorn. The handful of bathers already in the pool turned to stare.

"I'm not bathing in front of people," Tris said, crimson-faced. "I thought you had private baths, like in the girls' dormitory. It's not decent." *And they'll torment me because I'm fat*, she added silently.

"*I* can't wash in the same water as *kaqs*," objected Daja. "I *can't*."

The two women looked at Sandry, who shrugged. She was used to all kinds of bathing customs. In Hatar, the sexes washed together in large pools like these.

Rosethorn tapped a foot. She seemed about to speak, and not happily. Lark stopped her with a hand on her arm. "I'll show them where the private tubs are," she said gently. "Come on, girls."

Daja scrubbed in quiet misery. If her family had seen her at Frostpine's, they would not have stopped at the whippings they'd given her in the past, when she was caught watching metalsmiths. They might have declared her *trangshi* themselves. "Traders trade – they don't *do*," her mother had told her time after time. "We don't *handle*, we don't *work*. We pay *lugsha* the lowest price we can get for work, then sell it at the highest profit. It's all right to smile, listen to their tales, compliment them on their craft, if it means closing the trade. It is not all right to show an interest on our own account."

I'm so confused, Daja thought, drying off. *I don't know what's right any more. I don't even have anyone to* tell *me what's right.*

Maybe I must work it out for myself. And how am I supposed to do that?

CHAPTER SIX

When the porridge came to him the next morning, Briar took a ladleful, placed it in his bowl, looked at the result, then added another. No one scolded him, or took the pot away. He considered adding more, and decided not to push his luck. He was still trying to see what was allowed, and what wasn't.

Once Lark and Rosethorn asked the blessing, he began to eat greedily.

"Slow down," Sandry told him, soft-voiced. "It's bad for your digestion to eat so fast."

"Leave me be. I eat how I want to eat," he grumbled.

Shaking her head, Sandry picked up the honey pot, and added a large spoonful to his bowl. "You need the sweetening," she informed him.

"Give him the whole pot, then," murmured Daja.

Lifting the pitcher, its sides beaded with damp from the cold-box, Sandry poured milk on to Briar's food. "And that helps, too. You look like you need all the honey and milk you can stand."

Briar glared at her, offended. "Did I ask you to stick your neb in my life?"

She gave him an extra-sweet smile that Daja recognized instantly as being Sandry at her contrariest. "You didn't, but that's all right. I'll do it anyway. I'm like that."

He was about to swear at her, but the look in her bright eyes made him think twice. She was like no one he'd met in his life, this girl-Bag. If he yelled at her, he had the sneaking suspicion that she might give as good as she got.

"Well, if we're going to be *fancy*." Standing, Rosethorn went into her workshop.

Briar inspected the white and gold on top of his cereal, stirred everything gingerly, and tasted the result. Temple porridge had been good before – not like the thin slop he'd scrounged at home – but now it was rich and sweet. He told himself that nicked food tasted better, but he knew it was a lie.

Rosethorn came back with a twist of heavy paper. Carefully she sprinkled brown dust into everyone's bowls, and added more to the pot before she sat. "This is cinnamon – it comes from the eastern caravans. Dedicate Crane *tries* to grow the trees in his greenhouse, but he isn't succeeding." She grinned as she stirred the powder into her breakfast.

When the boy tasted the addition, he began to shovel food into his mouth as fast as he could swallow. Sandry opened her mouth to protest, then gave up.

"I don't see why you and Crane can't declare a truce, Rosie," complained Lark. "You liked each other once."

"Before he decided to play tricks on plants," retorted the other woman. "He treats their need for the change of seasons like – like a parent who thinks his child's love of a favourite blanket is babyish, so he takes the blanket away. Crane acts as if plants are wasting their time during autumn and winter."

"Plants *need* to die?" asked Briar, startled.

"Don't talk with your mouth full," snapped Rosethorn. "They need to *rest*. It's not the same thing." Taking his empty bowl, she ladled in more porridge. "Well, he's underfed," she said defensively to Lark, who watched her with a knowing smile.

After breakfast, all of them set about doing their scheduled chores. Briar was saved from having to admit he couldn't read the marks Lark had made on the big slate by Lark herself, who showed him how to scrub the cottage's small privy. For a change Briar had no thought of abandoning the work or even of doing it badly; he had plenty to think about that morning. Chief in his thoughts was the small tree he had seen not only the day before, but in his dreams as well.

When he returned to the cottage, the girls were finishing up their own chores. Rosethorn had gone into her workshop and closed the door – Briar could hear the sound of a sweeping broom in there. Lark was reading a message-slate that had been brought to her by one of the Temple's runners.

"As soon as you're finished, you're all to meet Niko at the Hub," Lark told the four. "Go straight there, mind – no side trips along the way." Digging in her pocket, she produced one of the round iron tokens that indicated they were allowed to roam, and tied four short threads around the hole at the top of it. She handed it to Daja. "Stay together. Remind Niko that you're to come back here for midday."

Daja raced upstairs to get her staff. "I like carrying it," she told Sandry, who eyed it with distaste. "It prevents misunderstandings."

"Walking with *girls*," Briar grumbled as the four ambled down the spiral road. "*Respectable* girls. I can't never show my face in Sotat again."

"You're just complaining to be complaining," Sandry pointed out. "We haven't done anything to you."

"Yet," he retorted, and fell silent.

Five boys from his old dormitory approached them on the road. One of them was the youth who'd claimed he'd stolen his cloak-pin. Inside his pockets, Briar's hands doubled into fists.

"It's the thief," sneered one boy.

"A thief and a Trader," added another, holding his nose. "Which is the lowest, do you think?"

Daja shifted her staff until she gripped it with both hands. She wouldn't start a fight, but she wouldn't put up with nonsense, either.

"A thief's a thief," said Cloak-Pin icily. "It doesn't matter if you call it that or 'Trader'."

Sandry grabbed Briar and Daja by the elbow. "Don't do anything!" she hissed. "They're not worth the trouble it takes to blow them from your noses."

"I don't need a keeper," hissed Briar, yanking away from her.

"Who's your play-pretty, thief-boy?" Cloak-Pin demanded.

"Who's the fatty?" muttered one of the others. Tris went pale.

"They let just anyone into the Circles, don't they?" jeered the boy who disliked Traders. He threw the core of an apple he'd been eating at Tris, and made oinking sounds.

Suddenly the air went cold. Something tightened around and inside the children in the blink of an eye. A faint crackling filled their ears.

"That's what this is!" cried Cloak-Pin, his eyes bright and gleeful. He didn't seem to feel anything odd. "A herd of pigs! A small herd, maybe, though Fatty and the Trader show promise..."

The hair rose on Sandry's arms. "Tris, no!" she hissed, feeling somehow that Tris was the source of the weirdness in the air.

"Let's get out of here." Daja grabbed one of Tris's arms, holding her staff up as a warning for the boys to keep their distance.

Briar grinned savagely, and put a hand under each arm, where he'd once carried two knives. After last night's bath, Niko had taken them all, but these bleaters couldn't know that.

At last the youths seemed to realize that something was not right. They backed off nervously. Quickly the four from Discipline took a path that cut across the loops of the road. Sandry and Briar stayed close to Tris, who was now pouring sweat. Only when they'd put two gardens between them and the boys did they slow down.

"Why did we do that?" Briar came to a halt in front of the girls, hands on hips. "We could've had a nice tumble, taught them some respect."

"I don't know *why* we did it." Daja leaned on her staff, and wiped her own sweating face on her sleeve. "I just had an idea that we had to."

Sandry dug in her belt-purse, until she found a small glass vial with a silver filigree cap. Opening it, she thrust it under Tris's nose.

Until that moment, the other girl had been staring into space, her pupils shrunk to pin-points, her face sickly white. When the fumes from the smelling-salts burned her nose, she gasped, and sneezed. As she groped for her handkerchief, the feeling of something stretched much too tight faded from the air.

"I – I got mad, didn't I?" she whispered.

"We *all* got mad," said Briar.

Tris looked at each of them frantically. "Did anything happen? Hail, or wind, or –"

"No," retorted Briar, shoving his hands into his pockets. "And I'da felt better for a proper tumble. *Girls.*"

"Nothing?" whispered Tris, clutching Sandry's arm. "*Nothing* happened?"

Sandry shook her head and returned the smelling-salts to her pouch. She'd forgotten she had them, until now. *I'd better keep them handy – just in case*, she told herself. In case of what, she refused to think.

Niko met them in front of the Hub and led them through the main doors. When Briar turned toward the kitchens, the man grabbed his arm and pulled him in the opposite direction, to an enclosed circle of beautifully carved wood. Inside, a wide stair wound through the tower's heart. Holding the door, Niko gestured for the boy to start walking down. Sandry, Daja and Tris followed.

As the staircase door closed behind them, all four halted, and looked around.

"It feels odd in here," Sandry whispered, without knowing exactly why. It wasn't frightening-odd, as when the boys had teased them – it was more pure, more soft. Briar scratched his suddenly-tickling scalp. Tris frowned. Daja ran a hand over the beautifully carved wall, and flinched; for a moment the wood had felt alive. Biting her lip, she touched it again. This time it felt like nothing more than wood polished until it was as smooth as glass.

"The staircase is spelled," Niko told them quietly. "The magical power in the Hub is so great that each part of the tower must be shielded from the others, to keep the different magics from bleeding into each other. In terms of magic, this is the cleanest place in all Winding Circle. You're having your first lesson in meditation here."

"Why?" Sandry wanted to know. "We'd be more comfortable at Discipline."

"Today we sacrifice comfort for security," replied Niko. "Every creature has magic, even if it's just the magic of life. In meditation, you open your mind – any magic you have spills out. By learning to concentrate here, any power you release will *stay* here, without affecting anyone else."

"What's magic got to do with me?" demanded Briar. "If I have any, it don't bother me." Daja nodded; Sandry and Tris both looked troubled.

"That's all very well and good, my boy," Niko said drily, "but have you ever thought that *you* might bother magic?"

Briar goggled at him.

"Make yourselves comfortable." Niko picked a spot on the ground floor landing, and sank into a tailor's seat. The others each chose a step. "We've only an hour – I couldn't arrange to keep this floor empty for any more time than that – so let's begin."

It was familiar to Tris at least, particularly since she had tried it again before going to sleep the night before. One thing was different: instead of breathing with the sound of waves, they counted as a way to time each step. Listening to Niko's soft instructions, the four inhaled as they counted to seven, held the breath as they counted to seven, and released it, counting to seven. They did this over and over, not even noticing when Niko stopped counting aloud for them.

When his leg cramped, Briar opened his eyes, examining the wood of the staircase. Niko was talking quietly, explaining how they must pull their minds from the entire staircase into something small. That was easy for the boy; right in front of him, someone had fitted a many-petalled rose into the carving. Shutting his eyes, Briar felt the change physically as he sank into the rose, petal by petal. Sandry placed herself in the wool fed to a drop spindle, feeling herself grow tight and thin and long as she spun herself into thread. Daja squeezed into the rounded striking surface of a fuller, and locked her mind on the warmth of hammering cherry-red iron.

"I believe that will do for one day." Niko sounded very pleased.

As if waking up, the four opened their eyes. For a moment they all felt cramped and knotted up, as if they had been pressed into small, tight balls. As they moved, the pain of stiff legs made them feel like themselves again.

Niko got to his feet and shook out his over-robe. "Now, I want to take you on a tour of the Hub, while we're here." He led them down the stairs, deep into the earth. At the bottom, he opened a small door.

Inside lay an immense, circular room with rock walls and a dirt floor. Torches provided most of the light. At the centre of the room, a fire with no fuel burned in a shallow pit, watched over by four dedicates – one in the green of Earth, one in the yellow of Air, one in Fire-red, the last in Water-blue. They said no word; they didn't move. The fire held their attention.

The children's skins prickled. It was hard to breathe. Old, patient strength filled the room, the strength of magic built and tended for centuries. Ghosts whispered, saying things none of them quite understood. Daja heard metal call from underfoot; kneeling, she found pieces of black, glassy rock embedded in the dirt. Briar heard the roots of plants, twining around each other to form a giant net. Tris felt the shift of rock, and the trickle of water between stones. Air pressed on Sandry. For a moment she thought that she stood on the whorl-wheel of the biggest drop spindle in the world. *And perhaps I do*, she thought, startled. *With the Hub to serve as the shaft, all Winding Circle is shaped just like a drop spindle.*

Niko stood by the wall, motioning for them to join him. Tris glanced at the four dedicates by the fire. They never moved. Since they wore their habits with the hoods up, and their hands were tucked into their sleeves, she couldn't be sure that they were alive.

"This is the heartfire – the true centre of Winding Circle," Niko whispered. "There are magics which keep this temple city whole, drained, fertile – without them, the bowl in which it rests would be a lake. All of those spells end in the heartfire chamber, and they are protected by those who guard the fire."

"What is that glassy stuff in the floor?" Daja asked. "It seemed – funny."

"It's not of this world." Kneeling, the man ran his fingers over a shiny piece of stone. "Thousands of years ago, a rock from the stars crashed here, leaving the crater where this place is built. The stones are its remains. Their magical power can be used for many things. They made it possible for Winding Circle's builders to anchor complex protective spells here without their affecting the magical work done afterwards."

Standing, he led them out of the room and up the stairs. Once they reached the ground floor and continued to climb, they could see that the stairs curved around open space, where vertical rope cables were strung. Above, something rattled. A set of ropes began to move, carrying an open box down before their eyes. Insides were five slates.

"That's how information coming into the upper floors is passed to Honoured Moonstream and the individual temples," Niko explained. "The dumbwaiter carries the slates to the ground floor, where runners pick them up."

"I saw no runners when we came in," Daja pointed out.

"They waited outside, until we had finished meditating," answered Niko. "They would have found us – distracting."

"What's that supposed to mean?" demanded Briar.

Sandry guessed, "It's the thing Niko said, about us spilling magic?"

Niko smiled and nodded. "That's exactly it." He brought them to a halt on a landing. Opening the door to the staircase, he beckoned for his students to look into the room beyond. It was a broad, airy chamber, its curved walls fitted with open, unshuttered windows. There were small tables, stacked with slates and chalk, placed in front of comfortable chairs. Only five chairs were occupied, by men and women in different-coloured habits, all with a black stripe along the hems. These dedicates sat back, eyes closed, ignoring the breezes that plucked at their clothes and hair.

Novices in white patrolled noiselessly, checking the table before each occupied chair. One found writing on a slate beside an elderly man in blue. Picking it up, the novice padded over to the door. The children stood aside to let her pass. Leaning over the rail, she tugged a rope.

Niko led the way up the stairs once more. "That is the place of hearing," he explained. "Those initiates—"

"What's an ini-whatsit?" asked Briar.

"You saw the black stripes on their habits? That means they are initiated into the methods of temple magic. They listen to the winds for voices, and report—"

Tris stumbled, and fell. Daja hauled her up. "What's the matter with you, merchant girl?"

"They hear voices on the winds?" Grey eyes feverish, Tris

grabbed Niko's arm. "They hear people *talking*?"

"From every imaginable location," he said.

"They really hear voices? *Really?* They don't just make up things, or – or hear what isn't there?" The other children stared at her.

"*You* hear voices?" Niko demanded sternly. "What do they speak of?"

"They – plenty of things. Shipping, weather. Sometimes booty, cow disease..." She blushed. "Sex. My family said I was crazy, or lying, or cursed..."

Sandry wrapped an arm around Tris, and glared at the mage as if this were his fault.

"Your family was mistaken," he said, smoothing his moustache. "The voices of madness are more interesting than what you've heard. From now on, tell me *anything* that you see or hear this way, understand? It may be important."

Tris gulped in air, getting herself under control. Only when she felt better did she step out of Sandry's hold.

"Come on," Niko ordered, when it was clear she was all right. The five of them started climbing again.

The seeing room, on the next level, looked much like the hearing room, except that dedicates here looked into bowls of water, or crystals, or mirrors, and the windows were covered with precious glass. Above that was the bird-cote, where messenger birds came and went from all around the Pebbled Sea. Higher up was the great clock that set the rhythm of Winding Circle's hours. The four would have stayed there all day if they could, watching the huge gears turn. Niko finally had to shoo them out, reminding them that it would soon be midday.

When they reached the ground floor, he stopped them from opening the door to the staircase. "Practice the trick I taught you – the pulling-in, becoming small – whenever you can. See if you can do it without having to meditate first. You all know me well enough to be aware that I don't ask things without a good reason."

"Then what *is* the reason?" Sandry wanted to know.

For a moment she thought that he was actually going to answer her, but he seemed to think the better of it. "I'd prefer not to go into it just yet," he said regretfully. "Some things will be easier for each of you if you work through them yourselves first."

There was a rolling boom; the ground quivered beneath them. The clock overhead continued to strike, telling the community and the surrounding farms that it was midday.

"Now, back to Discipline. Tris, I'll come for you after the rest period. We have more work to do," Niko said, opening the staircase door. "And all of you practise your meditation!"

Once the midday meal was over, Briar climbed the stairs to the attic. On his first day here, he'd found a trap door in the ceiling – now he pulled down the ladder beneath it, undid the latch, and crawled on to the roof. Seated on its peak, his back resting against the stone chimney, he could watch Rosethorn toil below. She worked among flowers today, passing up the afternoon rest period.

This is living, he thought. No Thief-Lord to hound him for more loot; he was fed, warm, dry, and lazing on a fragrant straw bed. The wealth of grey clouds rolling across the sky meant that the sun wasn't likely to burn him. Rain was coming, but not for a while. What he needed was a nap.

The moment he closed his eyes, the image of the ailing greenhouse tree entered in his mind. Rosethorn had wanted to see it, but he had a feeling Crane would not want to show it to her. Rosethorn might not even want to look at the tree if she knew it was one of Crane's.

Nap, he told himself firmly. *Them that know plants are looking after the tree.*

Something crunched nearby. He looked; the merchant girl was climbing on to *his* roof. He scowled. "Just because we live together doesn't mean I like you. Go away."

"I have the right to be here," Tris snapped. "More, because my room's just below."

"I didn't come out to be hearing girl bibble-babble," he warned.

"I'm not *bothering* you. Go back to whatever you're doing, and let me be!" She clambered over the roof's peak and settled on the other side, where he couldn't see her. Briar leaned back too hard and fast, and banged his spine on the rocks of the chimney. Wincing, he sat up. Any moment she would chatter, that was certain. He'd be drifting into a little nap, and she'd start asking questions about where he came from and what he did to get here.

Silence.

He fidgeted. Why *didn't* she say something? Was there ever a girl who didn't talk her teeth out? Certainly that Sandry had a mouth that ran on fiddlesticks.

Silence.

She had to be asleep. The moment she woke, she'd start bothering him.

Briar leaned back against the chimney, with more respect for its bumps than the last time, and closed his eyes. There, in his mind, clear as anything, was that sick tree. He opened his eyes with a muttered curse, and returned to worrying about the merchant girl.

Time passed, in silence.

The suspense was killing him. He crawled to the peak of the roof, and looked over. There she lay, hands behind her head, staring at the sky.

"What are you doing?" he asked.

Tris blinked. All through the meal and clean-up, she'd been thinking of deep breaths like sea-waves, and of pulling her mind into one small spot. Once she was settled on the thatch, her lungs fell into the breath-pattern easily. When Briar interrupted her this time, she was so deeply calm that she didn't mind.

"Watching a storm get born," she told him.

The boy frowned. He'd seen folk hypnotized at a fair, made to do silly things by the mage who put them in a trance. When they spoke, they sounded just like her. "Storms don't get born," he scoffed. "They're just there."

"You aren't looking right," she replied, still peaceful. "See? We're in a spot where you can watch clouds grow."

He looked up, but it was hard on his neck. "They just look like clouds."

"Wait. Pick a small one, and keep an eye on it. It helps if you do that breathing thing Niko taught us."

He squinted, but his neck refused to bend at that angle. Directing a scowl her way – not that she saw anything but the view overhead – he lay down on his side of the roof, just over the peak, and did as she suggested. Slowly he drew breath in, counting, then held it, then let it go. The sound of air moving through his lungs made him think of the breezes that ran over the thatch. He focused on the thickening clouds.

Briefly they looked as they always did, scudding across the sky like fat guild leaders who were late for important appointments. Then he saw a wisp put out a small bloom of grey, then another, and a third. Before it left the range of his vision, the wisp had blown itself into a medium-sized cloud, and was working on turning itself into a tall thunderhead.

"How do they do that?" He picked a new cloud. "It's like they create themselves."

"I don't know," she replied. "Maybe Niko will tell me."

"Why are they grey?"

"They have rain in them. We'll have a storm in an hour or so."

"How do you know?"

There was no answer.

"I don't see how a girl can know about storms."

She didn't reply, but neither did she get up and leave. He was startled to realize that he didn't want her to. She actually wasn't much trouble – for a merchant girl.

From its room atop the Hub, the clock sounded a deep note. The midday rest was over.

"Boy!" an imperious voice called from below.

There was a rustle of thatch. Tris crawled over the peak of the roof, bound for the trap door. "I was just getting comfortable," she complained.

"Then why leave?" he asked sensibly.

"Because I'm supposed to see Niko, remember?"

"Boy, I know you're up there!" Briar peered over the roof's edge. Rosethorn stood in the path, where she could see him. Raising a hand, she beckoned, an evil grin on her face. "Come down. You're going to help me prepare for this storm!"

He blinked. That was work...

Maybe she'll tell me the names of things, he thought.

He paused, not wanting to seem too eager, and thought of a grievance. "Briar!" he yelled at her.

"What?" called Rosethorn.

"My name is Briar! Not 'boy', *Briar*!"

"I know perfectly well what your name is, boy. Come on – I want to finish before it starts to rain!"

"It's *Briar*," he muttered, and followed Tris down into the house.

CHAPTER SEVEN

For a moment, Sandry thought she would cry. The wool that she had started to card after lunch was now a snarled mess. The process was simple. She'd done it as recently as a year ago: lay a clump of fleece on each card, then drag the teeth on one card through the wool on the other. The metal teeth groomed the clumps into fine, even strips of wool, to be coiled into rolags. Instead, her fibre escaped the cards, or yanked free of the teeth, or decided to cling to her. Had it still been attached to sheep, she would have suspected them of frisking. Worse, the air was close, hot and sticky – everywhere that wool touched her skin, she itched.

She'd thought that Lark couldn't hear her, over the clack of the loom, but the moment she sniffed, the woman stopped her work. "What's the matter?"

"It won't come *right*," Sandry replied, trying not to whine. "It's worse than ever, and it clings to everything! Why is it being so bad today?"

"Bring it here."

The girl obeyed, offering the messy cards to Lark.

"Mila preserve us, you look like you've grown a fur coat."

"When I try to pick it off, it just goes somewhere else." Sandry frowned at the ivory-coloured tufts on her dress and hands.

"It just likes you too much. You have to teach it to mind you." Lark pinched her fingers together, then pulled them back. Instantly the wool on Sandry stood on end, like dogs begging for a treat. An eerie prickling told the girl that the fibres on her cheeks were doing the same thing. "What I expected," the woman said. "Take a deep breath..."

Eyes closed, Sandry obeyed. Automatically she breathed as Niko had taught them that morning, counting to herself. Lark said quietly, "Pinch your fingers together over your dress, without touching it, then pull them away from you. Pinch with your mind as well."

With my mind? the girl thought, startled.

But surely that was the same as imagining herself as a tight thread. She made her mind into grasping fingers, and pinched with them, then opened an eye to see what had happened. A third of the wool fibres stood, wavering. The rest lay flat on her dress, crawling away from the spot that Lark had called them to.

"Really *want* it, Sandry. There should be nothing you want more just now."

Sandry closed her eyes, and *wanted* her mind to work with her fingers, to pull the fibres away from her dress. She peeked again. Now all of the wool had gone flat.

Lark chuckled. "Maybe you should order it, like most nobles order servants."

Just thinking of that made the girl smile grimly. She'd definitely seen enough of that kind of noble before! She snapped out her hand, as if she were Liesa fa Nadlen banishing Daja from the dining hall.

"We need to work on your control," she heard Lark say.

Sandry's eyes popped open. The bits of wool that had clung to her so hard had now jumped to Lark, and were huddled together on the dedicate's breast. Lark was grinning.

"I'm sorry!" cried Sandry. "I didn't – well..."

Lark patted her hand. "Don't frighten it. Wool hairs *want* to come together." She tried to pull the fibres off her clothes, without success. They were trying to weave themselves into her habit. "I'll need your help, since you are the one who did this," she told Sandry. "But *gently*."

The girl took up the pattern of breaths, until she was calm. There had been *something* when she had dismissed the wool, a feeling that was odd and yet familiar. She found it inside, and used it to call the fibres.

Softness tickled her palm: the wool now formed a small pile in her hand.

"There you go," Lark said approvingly as thunder rolled outside. "Now. Let me show you a charm that will keep it out of your face and off your dress."

Niko came for Tris when the storm was just beginning to make itself heard. She was pacing the main room nervously, wanting badly to go outside before the winds swept over the walls. When she saw Niko opening the small gate, she ran out to him.

"Put this on," he ordered, tossing her a long, oiled cape, the twin of the one that he wore. Once it was settled on her shoulders, he gave her a broad-brimmed hat just like his own to tie under her chin. The winds gusted through Winding Circle, tearing at curtains in windows and the clothes that they wore. In the gardens, dedicates and novices hurried to finish their work and get inside as the man and the girl walked briskly to the south gate.

Once outside Winding Circle, they picked their way down the cliff path and entered the cave. Small drops were already lashing the air. On the rocks below, the sea boomed, the waves foaming under the whip of the wind.

As she pushed back her hat, Tris squinted into the gloom. Lightning flared in long strips out to sea, throwing the world into relief. Curtains of rain parted. People had lit the beacons in the harbour lighthouses; they shone a warning to storm-caught ships and boats, to steer away from the rocky islands just off Summersea.

"Watch the lightning. Concentrate on it. Think about it," Niko yelled over a crash of thunder.

"What is it? Lightning, I mean?" Tris yelled back.

"Power builds in the sky and ground in a storm. The power in the ground strives to meet that which is in the clouds. When they connect, lightning shows the path the power takes. Never forget, all power *must* go somewhere once there's enough of it." Thunder growled around them, as if in agreement. "Thunder is air along the path. It heats so fast that the air booms like a drum." The roar of thunder faded. More quietly he said, "Now that you know what lightning is, concentrate! Try to feel where the next bolt will strike – feel for power building up."

"What if it decides to come after me?"

"It won't. Magic only attracts lightning when it's meant to, thank the gods, or those with magical power wouldn't live to be mages. Where will the next bolt strike?"

She watched the lightning pick its way across the sea, approaching the harbour islands. "I can't tell. It just goes any old where."

"Try!" He almost had to scream to be heard over a thunder-blast. "It's connected to you – feel for it!" His words rang clearly in the pause between cracks of thunder.

"Ouch," she grumbled, rubbing the ear he'd been yelling into.

"Your ear is fine," he snapped, grabbing the ear in one hand and twisting slightly.

"Niko!"

"Stop ducking the lesson. Tris, there's only so much that I, or anyone, can teach you. To control the power that makes your life so hard, you must be able to grasp it at any time, in any place. Let *nothing* stop you from bearing down, understand? Or do you want to kill someone one day, and only find out afterwards that you didn't mean to?"

She stared up at him, terrified. Lit by flickers of lightning, his eyes pits of shadow in his craggy face, he looked eerie. It was as if he knew all the dark places in her heart.

Lightning blazed. A single broad strip lanced into a tree on the peak of the rock that was Bit Island, and a hundred burning fragments flew through the air. Tris's gleeful shout was drowned in a thunder-crash that shivered her bones.

"A good thing it only struck a tree, and that tree alone on a rocky peak," Niko said when they could hear again. "Lightning creates hundreds of wildfires every year, burning acres of forest and croplands. It kills people and animals, too. It's a dangerous toy – keep that in mind."

"If it's so dangerous, why not push the storms out to sea – or better yet, stop them cold? I mean, *I'd* miss them, but wouldn't that be easier for most people?"

"Oh, no!" he said instantly. "Easy perhaps for the people, but it would mean death or madness for a mage." He waited for a growl of thunder to end before he went on. "Nature has her own power. Tempting as it is, mages should never tinker with Nature, not in a storm, or in an earthquake, or with the tides. She may allow it for a time, but eventually she always loses her temper. The results can be – devastating. Trust me."

He sighed. "Even the greatest mages have their limit – and Nature is it."

"But – aboard ship – those knots. The captain said *mimanders* tie the wind in those knots. Isn't that meddling with Nature?"

Niko smiled thinly. "*Mimanders* who specialize in winds spend their *lives* learning nothing else – those that survive apprenticeship, anyway. Just one in ten lives to be a journeyman, you know. As masters they coax the winds into thinking that the curves of the knot are the open lanes of air where they usually travel. Are you prepared to spend ten years or more learning to be a simple puff of air? Learning only that, and nothing else, and that only if you live?"

Tris stared out at the white-capped waves. The storm was moving on, the roll of thunder growing more distant. *There has to be a quicker way*, Tris thought. *If* I *was a mage, I'd get Nature to do my bidding. They'd call me "Storm-Killer," and I would be famous all over the world.*

Niko tugged her ear gently. "Let's try the exercise again. Breathe in..."

When Daja entered Frostpine's forge, the fire was banked. Only Kirel was there, up to his elbows in clay as he shaped moulds.

She hesitated. "I – was looking for Dedicate Frostpine?"

"Just walk around to the other side of this building. He's a goldsmith today."

Curious, Daja asked, "Shouldn't you be with him?"

Kirel grinned. "I'm only his apprentice for iron – he doesn't have an apprentice for his work in gold. Though he *did* mention he thought someone might come by to help him."

Daja thanked him, and circled the building. Looking through the door on the opposite side, she saw Frostpine. He stood at a counter with his back to her, in front of one of three upright metal rectangles. A series of holes were punched through each, in sizes that ranged from one that was nearly a third of an inch across in the leftmost plate, to one that was a pinpoint in the rightmost.

Using flat-ended tongs, he gripped a tongue of metal that protruded through the hole in the middle of the central plate. Lifting a foot to brace himself against the counter, he began to pull. Slowly, fraction by fraction, he drew gold wire from the hole.

"Daja – will you do me a favour?" he asked, voice strained.

She started. How did he know she was there again? "Um – what do you need?" She propped the staff beside the door, and went to him.

"On the other side of this plate, there's a coil of wire. Straighten it as I pull?"

She found the coil and picked it up; it was barely warm gold, and coarse to her touch. Obediently she opened a loop of it until a straight length fed into the metal plate. "What is all this?" she asked.

"I'm drawing gold wire." Lowering his foot, Frostpine continued to back up, without faltering. "Precious metals – they're soft, compared to iron. By greasing the wire with beeswax – dragging it through smaller and smaller holes – it gets thinner, and longer."

"It looks hard," she said, as the last of the gold fed through the plate. Frostpine turned his face away as the wire popped free. To Daja's horror, it snapped like a whip – if the man hadn't turned away, the flying end might have lashed his face.

Frostpine gathered the new wire, and took it to the

counter. First he rubbed cold beeswax over its length, then wound it into a coil. Choosing a smaller hole in the plate, he thrust the wire's pointed end into it. "It looks hard because I'm not putting my whole self into it. If I did..."

He closed his eyes and took a long breath. Briefly he held it, then let it go, slowly. Daja's skin prickled. Something even warmer than the summer air gathered in the room, to wind itself around the smith. Each piece of metal in the shop seemed to burn with inner fire. Something in her answered, timidly.

The man breathed as Niko had taught the children, then strode to the front of the plate to seize the wire's point with his tongs. This time he didn't brace himself; he only pulled, backing up. The metal flowed through the plate slowly first, then faster, as if half-liquid. Frostpine didn't turn away when the end popped out; he lifted his hand. The free end of the wire leaped into it.

"Physically it's easier this way." He gathered the new, thinner wire. "But it burns up my strength here" – he touched his chest – "and here." He patted his head. "I'd hate to get a nasty surprise and have nothing to fight it with." Examining the metal, he frowned. "This needs the fire again." He crossed the room, entering a small cubicle. Heat rippled through the open door; inside was a small forge. The only light came from its fire.

He placed the gold coil on the coals with tongs. Another, thicker length of wire was already there. This he lifted out.

"See that red colour? Your gold is just hot enough to be worked." Carrying the wire out of the cubicle, he put it on an anvil and turned it several times, as if he turned sausages in a frying pan. "The anvil draws the heat out. Any questions?"

She blinked. "Umm – no, sir."

"Then here." He rubbed beeswax on the new wire, then fed one narrow end through a hole in one of the plates. "The flat metal pieces are properly called 'drawplates', since this way of making wire is called 'drawing'." Taking Daja's arm, he placed his tongs in her hand, and folded her fingers around them. "These are draw-tongs – the flattened ends make it easier to grip the metal. Draw the wire."

She stared at the tool. "How?"

"Take a deep breath..." She did it as he raised his hand before her face. "Clear your mind. Let your breath out. Now, grab that end with your tongs, shut your eyes, and call the metal to you. When it feels right – mind that, it must *feel* right, not *look* right – start pulling. Don't stop. If you do, that makes a weak spot in the wire. Keep going till it's all the way through."

"I *call* it?"

Frostpine grinned, white teeth flashing. "Come, Trader-girl. You know gold, surely? You've held it, seen it in different forms. Think of gold in your innermost heart, and call it to you. Don't forget to pull on the wire as you call."

Thunder boomed outside.

Nervously, she walked to the front of the plate, and gripped the wire's end in her pincers. Call metal to her? It was metal, not a living thing...

Once, when she was small, she had crept into a goldsmith's shop. It was dark inside. Only the smith was visible, her body outlined in forge-fire. With tongs she had lifted a bottle from the coals. Turning until she held the bottle over a mould, she had tilted it. Living fire poured out in a yellow-white stream that sparkled and glittered as it fell.

Daja, eyes closed, called the memory of that flow, her arms straining. The metal fought her at first. She called it again in her heart. Slowly – a little at a time – that remembered gold turned away from the mould in her mind's eye, and reached out to her.

Catching her foot, she opened her eyes. She stood a yard from the drawplate. Her tongs gripped a wire three times longer than the piece that she had started with.

With a gasp, she dropped tongs and wire to the ground. "I'm sorry – I muffed it! I didn't take it through all the way. I weakened your gold," she said. Even her arms and knees felt weak and loose, trembling after so much effort. Had it taken an effort? Thunder boomed, almost overhead. She sat down on the floor, hard.

"Don't worry – that was just an experiment. Drink this." He put a stone cup filled with liquid under her nose. "It will put you to rights."

It tasted like water with mint leaves crushed into it. She drank it all, and found that she could get to her feet.

"You have a talent for this," Frostpine told her. "And any fool can see you love metalwork. Would you like to learn smithcraft? Come here, say, in the afternoon, after the rest period? I'd like to have the teaching of you."

"Can I?" she whispered. "No one will beat me, or lock me in my room, or make me do extra chores for being with *lugsha*? You'll *let* me learn?"

"It's more than just my *letting* you, Daja," Frostpine said, tweaking one of her braids. "I waited for years for someone who loves it as I do to come along."

Trembling, she stared up into his face. "If I hadn't..." The words caught in her throat. She tried again. "If our ship hadn't sunk, if I wasn't *trangshi* now..."

"Daja—"

She shook her head. "I would have gone all my *life*

thinking I was wrong. Thinking I was *dirty* to want to do *lugsha* things. Being a bad Trader. Being a bad Kisubo."

The man shook his head. Outside, rain whipped the air. "Don't blame your people. They live hard lives. Their beliefs help your people to stay together, to defend themselves against lords and merchant guilds."

"I know that," she admitted. "But how many Trader kids are like me, wanting to learn *lugsha* work?"

"'Kids'?" he asked with a smile.

"Something a boy I live with says."

"Well, 'kid'" – he winked, drawing a smile from Daja – "after we get well into things like charcoal, coal, different hammers and different tongs, you may think the Traders have the right of it after all." He put his hands on his hips and looked her over. "We start by finding you a proper apron. And you might consider wearing clothes you don't mind soiling. You're going to get very dirty at this."

A moment ago she would have been glad to reject anything Trader, like her scarlet mourning. Now she blinked with dismay. He was right, she knew he was, but... She smoothed her hand over a sleeve. She would ask Lark. Lark would know what to do.

Frostpine resettled his belt. "Kirel's aprons and mine are too big. We're off to the tanners'." Putting an arm around her shoulders, he steered her out into the rain.

Watching Briar and Tris bicker as they washed the supper dishes, Daja remembered Frostpine's instructions. It still bothered her to think of putting off her mourning, but she knew the smith was right. Scarlet clothes were too expensive. "Lark?" she asked, hesitantly. "I – there's a smith who'd like me for an assistant."

Lark had been about to rise from the table. She settled back into her chair instead. "Does he have a name?" she asked.

"Frostpine."

Lark and Rosethorn shared a look – an odd look, thought Sandry, who watched them with interest.

"Niko was right," murmured Rosethorn.

"We know Frostpine," Lark told Daja. "He's a good man, and a fine smith. You'll learn a lot from him. He wants to see you in the afternoons?"

Daja nodded. "Are there – do you know where I could find – well, other clothes?" She smoothed a hand over her scarlet tunic. "Nothing fancy, just – leggings, maybe, and some shirts."

Lark nodded. "That's sensible – it's no use getting your mourning all burned and streaked in the forge. I don't have leggings, but will breeches do?"

Daja nodded, looking at the table in front of her.

A warm brown hand rested on her shoulder. "I can make you a scarlet headband, and a scarlet armband, so you'll have some colours to wear for your family," Lark told her. "So people will know of your loss."

For a moment Daja couldn't speak past a lump in her throat. Lark had seen her heart. She knew what it cost to put aside the scarlet, and had offered a practical way not to. Now the Kisubo spirits would not be angry and take revenge, or think that she hadn't loved them. "Thank you," she whispered. "That is kind."

"Then let's take care of it right now." Lark took Daja upstairs, where general stores for the cottage filled boxes in the space between the girls' rooms. "These should fit you," she told Daja as she opened a crate. Sorting through folded clothes, she picked out several pairs of breeches – three in different shades of brown, one in leaf green, one in dark blue – and placed them in the girl's outstretched arms.

"With the weather turning hot, these should be suitable," Lark said, adding light, sturdy tunics in green, orange, light brown and blue to Daja's stack. "Why don't you try them all on? Those that don't fit, bring to me. I'll have the headband and armband for you by tomorrow."

"Thank you," Daja whispered, clutching an armful of clothes that smelled of cedar chips and sun-drying.

"It's hard to break traditional ways," Lark said kindly. "If it helps, the people of Caravan Qurilta wore headbands and armbands one year when they followed the Spice Trails into Aliput. There, all-scarlet clothes mean disease in the house."

Daja frowned. Hadn't she heard about that somewhere?

"I saw it with my own eyes," Lark said in Tradertalk, framing her eyes with two fingers. Among Daja's people that sign was as holy as a vow to Koma and Oti. "I rode with them when it happened. They'd lost the caravan-master and three of the guards in a rock slide."

"You lived with Traders?" Daja blushed; she hadn't meant to sound shocked.

"I wasn't always a housebird." Lark's eyes twinkled. "I belonged to a company of acrobats. We travelled to Yanjing to work and to learn their acrobats' tricks." Gently she pinched Daja's upper and lower lips with her fingers, to get the girl to close her mouth. "Have I shocked you with my disreputable past?"

Daja gasped. "Oh – Lark, no, no, I was just..." Looking at the woman's dancing eyes, Daja realized Lark had been joking.

"Your family won't hate you if you relax a bit, you know,"

the woman told her softly. "I think they'd want you to really live your life, *trangshi* or no."

Daja turned to take the clothes into her room, thinking about what Lark had said. A flicker of green – a cartwheel? – caught her eye. She looked back, to see Lark turn a second cartwheel before she went down the stairs.

The woman looked back and up at her. "And I'm not completely a housebird yet," she said, and winked.

Smiling, Daja went into her room to try on her new things.

CHAPTER EIGHT

That night Tris slept deeply, without dreams. When the voices got her attention just after dawn, she was already awake, feeling more rested than she had in a long time. For a moment she cringed, afraid of still more evidence that she was losing her mind. Then she remembered what Niko had told her. The voices weren't signs of insanity – he wanted to know what they said to her.

"Quick! There he..."

"No, that way! Circle him!"

"It's that cursed thief-boy!"

Tris rolled off the bed and thumped her knees. She scrabbled under the bed for her shoes.

"Be careful of that tree!" the voice cried. "It's a Yanjing *shakkan*, and priceless, priceless!"

Tris lurched out the door and headed for the stairs. Banging her ankle on a crate, she yelped.

Daja opened her door, yawning. "I didn't hear Lark call. What are you doing?"

"Collecting bruises," Tris muttered, and limped down the stairs.

Sandry too was up and dressed, clumsily slicing bread at the table. "What is it?"

Tris ran out the front door. Once she was in the open, the clamour of distant voices reached her ears clearly.

"Will you *please* tell me what it is?" Sandry had followed her.

Looking for the sources, Tris pointed them out. Dedicates in yellow and novices in white approached at the run, along the spiral road and between the loomhouses across from the cottage. Racing towards Discipline, something cradled against his chest, was Briar.

Sandry ran to the low gate, and opened it. Waving frantically, she beckoned to him.

"Stop, thief!" A lean dedicate, his yellow habit hemmed in black, led the group on the spiral road. "You, girl!" he cried, panting and red-faced from the effort of running, "Don't you *dare* help him!"

"Why *are* we helping you?" Tris enquired as Briar stumbled past her.

"Stuff yourself," he snapped. "I never asked for help!"

Sandry closed the gate, and latched it firmly, grim-faced. It wasn't much of a barrier, but it was better than nothing. Deliberately she stepped into the middle of the path, putting herself squarely between hunters and prey. A breeze caught her black gown and veil, making them wave like banners.

"Admit me instantly!" cried the dedicate who appeared to be the leader, when he reached the gate. The order lost its force as he braced his hands on his knees and gasped for breath.

A novice reached over the gate to feel for the latch. He jumped back when the girl slapped his hand. "I did not give you permission to come on to my home ground," Sandry cried, eyes blazing. "I *forbid* you to enter!"

Tris's jaw dropped as she thought, *She is either crazy, or the bravest person I've ever met.*

"Little girl, rank means nothing here!" snapped the novice. He tried to reach the latch again. Sandry doubled her fists and stepped up to the gate.

"What is going on?"

Tris hadn't thought a time might come when she would be glad to see Rosethorn, but she was now. The dedicate had clearly been at work in the gardens: her green, dew-soaked habit was kilted up, showing legs streaked with dirt; a broad-brimmed straw hat sat on her cropped auburn hair. Coming out of the house, she kept Briar at her side with an arm wrapped firmly around his shoulders. Daja and Lark brought up the rear, Daja carrying her staff.

"Don't play innocent," snapped the dedicate who had bent over. He straightened, his long face the colour of a ripe plum. "Since you are barred from *my* greenhouse, you sent this young rodent..."

"Roach," muttered Briar.

"Shut up, boy," Rosethorn said through clenched teeth.

Briar's accuser crossed his arms. "Your *spy* stole a one-hundred-and-thirty-year-old *shakkan* tree, and I *demand* its return!"

"I do *not* have spies, Crane, you idiot. And you couldn't tend a *shakkan* properly if your life depended on it. You set plants in that glass monstrosity of yours and expect them to skip the pattern of seasons because *you* ask them—"

"Please, everyone, disharmony upsets the balance of the Circle." Lark came forward, dark eyes grave. "Dedicate Crane, Rosethorn would no more steal a plant from you than you would steal one of hers. *I* know that, if you do not."

Tris noticed Crane's instant blush, and wondered if he hadn't tried to take something of Rosethorn's once or twice.

Lark continued, "If she *did* want to steal anything of yours, we also know that she would take it herself, not send a deputy."

"Thanks, Lark," Rosethorn said with a one-sided grin.

Crane was not to be silenced. "He is a thief! He stole from a lad at the boys' dormitory—"

"I never!" cried Briar. "That brooch was junk—"

"Hush," Lark ordered.

"*Anybody* could see that!" finished Briar. To Lark he whispered, "I got my pride."

"He was found innocent by the Air temple's own truth-sayer," Rosethorn snapped. "In the presence of Moonstream herself."

"Is he innocent *now*?" demanded Crane. More dedicates and novices who should have been at the dining hall joined the group behind him, listening with interest. "Tell me he didn't steal my *shakkan*!"

"It's *sick*," Briar told Lark and Rosethorn. "Whatever he's doing, it's not helping!"

"I want my *shakkan*, and I want that *thief* cast out!" snapped Crane. "He doesn't belong here! As soon as you return my *property*, Moonstream will hear my complaint!"

"Shame on you!" cried Lark, gold-brown cheeks flushed. "Who are *you* to judge who is fit to stay or go? This lad is here for a *reason*!"

Briar rubbed the bowl in which the tree was planted with shaky fingers. If they threw him out, he would go dry and dead himself.

Rosethorn tapped his shoulder. Looking up, he met her brown eyes squarely. *Please*, he thought, praying that she could read his mind. *Please*.

Rosethorn faced her rival. "A tomato plant," she said abruptly. "Let the boy – and the *shakkan* – go, and you can have one of my tomato plants."

"With a few words on it so it will die once I transplant it?" Dedicate Crane flapped a scornful hand. "Thank you, no!"

Rosethorn sighed. "With a few words on it so it will *prosper* with you, Crane. Though once you force it to harvest out of season, the fruits won't taste the same."

"So *you* say," was the angry retort. "One plant in exchange for a *shakkan*? You insult me."

"Why don't we talk inside?" Lark suggested. Glancing at the crowd of onlookers, she said, "I know that service at the dining hall will be over soon" – instantly a few dedicates and all of the novices hurried away – "and some of us here would like to prepare our *own* meal."

Briar and the girls were sent to their rooms as the dedicates talked. Strain his ears though he might, Briar could hear none of the conversation. He gave up trying to listen, and put the tree on his window sill. It was a pine, he knew that much. But how did it get this small? With a finger, he traced the curve of the trunk: it grew sharply to the right. The branches had a kind of poetry about them, as if they had been made to grow in just that way.

"I'll say this for you..."

He gasped, flinched, and almost knocked his prize over. Grabbing it, he faced Rosethorn. She lounged against his door, which she had closed.

"...you don't pick the easy path. Calm down, I'm not going to arrest you."

"Are you going to make me give it back?"

"That depends. Who'll take care of that thing? *Shakkans* – particularly sick *shakkans* – require work. Even a healthy one demands attention – they're as vain as a plant can be, after decades of being tended. I'm a busy woman."

Carefully, gently, Briar placed the tree on his sill once more. "If – if someone could tell me what to do, I – I'd like..."

He gulped. "There's no way it can be a hundred and thirty years old!"

Rosethorn sighed. "Yanjing gardeners took a thousand years to develop the art of miniature trees," she explained. "If a seed or clipping agrees to it – and it *must* agree – the gardeners trim the roots and branches, and wire the trunks and limbs. It's all to make them grow in a shape that concentrates each plant's strength." She walked over, and cupped the *shakkan*'s bowl in her palms. "However it's done, they're works of art, as much as a tapestry or a statue. And this one is not a hundred and thirty. It's a hundred and forty-six – ask it yourself."

Briar scowled, thinking she was teasing him – except that, come to think of it, she didn't tease anyone.

"I'll teach you how to care for it," Rosethorn told him. "It's not the kind of project I would select for a beginner, but since the tree chose *you*..."

"How could it choose me? It doesn't even know me."

Rosethorn shook her head. "One reason there are *shakkans* – apart from their being so beautiful – is because they can store magic. They *become* magic. It enables them to call to those who will do them the most good."

Briar looked at the tree with new respect. "I hope you don't end up sorry for calling me," he told it. "I don't know from anything. Ask *her*."

"As for this room," Rosethorn said, "this is not what I would call properly cleaned. Your blankets and pillow belong on *their* proper place – the bed."

"I don't sleep there," complained Briar. "It's too high up. What if there are rats under it? They'll chew through them leather straps holding it up and they'll get me when I fall."

"Oh, for—" Rosethorn snapped, impatient. She stopped,

took a breath, and said more gently, "No rat would dare show itself here. If this worries you, though, we'll get rid of the bedstead. You can have the mattress on the floor. And *that* bed you will make up properly, starting right now."

"But..." he protested as she went to the door. "My tree – and – breakfast..."

"That tree waited the months Crane had it to come to you; it can wait until this afternoon for us to work on it."

As she went out, Briar started to gather his bedclothes.

The residents of Discipline were eating breakfast when Tris asked, "I'd've thought you'd wait till no one was around before you stole something."

The boy gulped his plum juice. "I thought they were still in bed," he said, blushing. "Instead they were sitting in the middle of that greenhouse thing where I couldn't see them, chanting."

"Renewing the quake spells on the glass," guessed Lark. "With all the earth-tremors, it stands to reason."

Briar shrugged. "I was quiet, and I kept out of sight, but..."

Rosethorn lifted an eyebrow. "You've never heard of alarm spells?"

"Bags have 'em, sure, but this wasn't no Baghouse."

Lark coughed, and scratched at her plate with her fork. "Dedicate Crane – Dedicate *Initiate* Crane – is a former Bag," she explained. "Perhaps that is why he is so mistrustful as to place alarm spells in a temple city. Who's he related to, Rosethorn?"

"Count Albannon fer Yorvan," the other woman replied. "It's in Olart," she added when the four looked at her.

"Bags," grumbled the boy in disgust. "They're all alike."

"Probably," Rosethorn agreed. "But listen well, Briar Moss. If you had tried to take a plant from *me*, I would have known – and *I* don't need alarm spells."

He looked at her, dismayed. "I never would!" he protested. "Never, *ever*!"

"Oh, *you*," grumbled the woman. "Eat. When rest period's over, we'll have a look at that bush you stole." She got up and went into her workroom.

Only when he was sure that she was out of hearing did Briar mutter, "It's a *tree*. A *shakkan* tree. Not a bush."

CHAPTER NINE

Lark pointed to the slate on the wall. "Chores. Do a good job today – there won't be time for it tomorrow. Daja, after you scrub the privy, ask Rosethorn for herbs to sweeten the air. Briar, don't neglect corners when you dust and sweep."

Everyone got to work. Even the dedicates swept out their workrooms, and cleaned the altar tucked in the corner between Sandry's room and the front door. Once they were finished, they vanished into their workrooms.

Pouring hot water into the tub where dishes awaited Sandry, Tris saw that Briar scratched at the floor with a broom. "No, no!" she called. "Dust first, *then* sweep. That way you get the dust you knock to the floor."

He looked at the broom and at the dustcloth. "You do?"

Tris went to Briar. "Here." She ran the cloth over a table, carefully doing the corners. Aunt Uraelle, who had kept her for three years, *always* checked her dusting, making her do it all over if she missed a spot. "Do flat surfaces this way. When the rag gets dirty, shake it out the window. Now you. There's a shelf."

The shelf that she pointed to held a few small objects. Briar nervously poked at the spaces between them with his cloth.

"No!" cried Tris. "You have to pick them up, and dust them, and do the shelf under them! Honestly, you'd think you never dusted in your life!"

"I haven't." *Who'd guess that people did things to keep*

their homes clean – or that they'd want clean homes in the first place? he thought.

"Me neither," called Sandry from the washtub.

Tris pushed her spectacles up on her nose. "But..."

"We had servants," explained the other girl.

Briar shrugged. "I didn't have a house. Maybe my dam had a room, but she died years ago. The Thief-Lord wasn't what you'd call a bear for housekeeping."

"Mila bless us!" Tris said. "Well, then, watch me." Carefully she lifted the vase that Briar had tried to work around, and dusted it. "See? And before you put it back..." She briskly ran the cloth over the spot where the vase had been, then returned it to its former position. Handing the cloth to the boy, she pointed to the dog statuette that was next on the shelf. "Now you."

Once he was dusting well enough to suit her, she went to the dishes that Sandry had washed, and began to rinse and dry them. Shaking her head, she muttered to the other girl, "No house! As well as live among savages!"

"We had fine tunnels underground," Briar remarked. His back was to them as he dusted, so he couldn't see Tris's glare. "If you didn't mind rats. My mate Slug, he trained a rat to bite the toes of merchant folk. You should've seen them jump! Smart rat, eh?"

"I don't think it's funny!" Tris told Sandry, who giggled helplessly. After that, she kept her opinions about Briar's upbringing to herself.

The boy grinned, and set about dusting the window ledges.

That morning Niko held their class in meditation at Discipline. Before they started, Lark and Rosethorn did an odd thing: they walked a circle around the cottage, Lark going clockwise, Rosethorn counter-clockwise. Lark carried a ball of white yarn, letting it unroll, until the yarn reached all the way around the house. At the front door, where she had started, she tied the ends together, so that it made a closed circle. Rosethorn carried a basket of dried herbs with her, and trickled a stream of them in her wake as she walked her own circle. When she finished, the dried leaves and stems formed another O that enclosed the cottage. Only then did she and Lark join everyone else in the main room.

"Why did you do that?" Sandry wanted to know.

"It's to keep magic from leaking in as we meditate," replied Niko.

Rosethorn muttered, "Or from leaking out."

"*Everyone*," Niko said, frowning at her, "breathe and count. One, two, three..."

The dedicates sat on the floor and performed the breathing exercise with the rest of them. Today it seemed easier for the children to bring their minds to a pinpoint of concentration. Niko looked genuinely pleased when they finished, and told them they had made real progress.

Going outside, Lark untied her yarn and rolled it up. Rosethorn followed. Scuffing her foot through the line of herbs in several places, she broke her circle.

During midday, Lark gave Daja a scarlet armband and a scarlet headband, to show that she was a Trader in mourning. Watching Daja put them on, Sandry looked at her own black clothes. Her mourning was not suited to housework or to carding and spinning wool. Even after she'd used Lark's wool-drawing charm, her overdress last night still had a fuzzy white coat.

She finished washing the midday dishes, then climbed the stairs. Her own boxes were neatly stacked in an attic corner. Opening them, she found her old, everyday summer gowns – a rose muslin and two blue ones, two brown linen dresses and undergowns in white or undyed cotton and linen. These were the things she had worn last year, plain clothes for travelling in. For a moment she hugged them, breathing in the sweet pea sachet that Pirisi had always tucked into her boxes.

Wiping a hand over her watering eyes – "So much *dust* up here," she muttered – she stripped off her black cambric overgown. The rose muslin went on in its place, and she sighed with relief. Light as the cambric had been, this was *much* more comfortable.

Once she was finished with her boxes, she looked around. The doors to Tris's and Daja's rooms were open – where had they gone? She didn't think they'd left the cottage.

Turning, she saw a ladder that led through an open trap door in the roof. She climbed it, to find the other two girls seated on the thatch. "It's still wet from the storm, isn't it?" she enquired.

Tris patted the canvas that she had brought to sit on. "Though if it keeps this hot, it'll be dry by tomorrow." Laying back, she linked her hands behind her neck.

Daja stood by the chimney, one arm around it as if it were a mast. Shading her eyes, she inspected Winding Circle. "Actually, this is a nice view," she remarked. "This whole place is built like a bowl. It's almost the same as the Amphitheatre of Heroes in..."

"Zakdin, Hatar." Sandry made a face.

Tris moved over, offering her a place on the canvas. She took it.

"Only there's no buildings or trees there," Daja went on.

Quietly Sandry told her, "There isn't an Amphitheatre any more, either. After the smallpox epidemic, they took all the bodies into it, then burned the whole thing. It was only made of wood."

Hurriedly Tris drew a gods-circle on her chest. "That's *horrible*," she remarked with a shudder.

Sandry tugged a straw out of the thatch. "When Niko and I left, the king was saying he'd rebuild it in marble."

"It should look nice," Daja said with approval. "White or black marble, did he say?"

Sandry's gloom lifted. "I forgot to ask," she replied with a tiny smile. "I still wasn't talking very much then."

"*Speaking* of you talking…" Daja came to share the canvas with them. "That novice won't forget you pulled rank on him, in front of Crane and everyone. Just like the girls from your old dormitory won't forget."

Tris opened a sleepy grey eye. "She did odd things in her old dormitory, too?"

"She took up for me," explained the Trader.

"Remind me to write them a note saying that I apologize," Sandry replied, tossing her braids back over her shoulders.

Daja shook her head. "Why get in the middle? Briar stole that tree, and it was costly. *Minimum* I ever saw a *shakkan* priced for was ten silver astrels."

Tris clicked her tongue against her teeth, impressed.

"I had to help," Sandry replied flatly. "He's one of us."

Daja blinked. "*Is* there an us?"

Sandry looked surprised. "Certainly! Didn't that thing this morning convince you?"

"I try not to let fights convince me of anything." Daja lay back.

"And I wasn't in it, not really," objected Tris.

“Oh, stop.” Sandry gave her a friendly push. “Why did you fetch help, if you didn’t care if they got him?”

Tris blushed scarlet, and held her tongue, not wanting to say that she’d half-hoped to see him in real trouble. Should she tell the others that he was at the foot of the ladder now, listening? The warm air that rose through the trap door from the house below carried the sound of his breathing to her sensitive ears.

“You’re getting ahead of yourself,” Daja said, yawning. “I don’t want to be an ‘us’ with a bunch of *kaqs*.”

“Or I with a Trader and a noble and a thief,” remarked Tris sleepily.

“You’ll see,” retorted Sandry. “I know what I’m talking about.”

From atop the Hub, the bell tolled the end of the rest period. Tris heard Briar tiptoe out of the attic as the girls got to their feet. Folding her canvas, she thought, *At least he’ll have the decency to pretend he didn’t hear any of that.*

“What are you and Niko doing today?” asked Sandry, descending the ladder. “Pass the cloth to me.”

Tris obeyed. “We’re going down to the cove,” she explained, climbing into the attic once Sandry had gotten off the ladder. “He mentioned something about learning tides. And I get to practise my meditation some more.”

“Good luck,” Sandry replied.

“Thanks,” Tris said, her voice very dry. “I’ll probably need it.”

Fretting, Briar watched as Rosethorn lifted his tree from the counter in her workroom. She cupped its small, round pot in her hands, dirt-stained fingers probing the openings in the bottom and testing each bump in the glaze.

"Why are there holes?" he asked, unable to keep still. "Won't the dirt fall out?"

"They let water drain through as it does in the ground. You put screens over the holes to keep dirt in. Now hush." Closing her eyes, Rosethorn ran her fingers over the earth in the pot, then over the surface twists that were part of the *shakkan*'s roots.

Briar's nose itched. The scent in that room, of black earth, herbs and flowers, of rain on hot stones, filled his ears and nose, tickling his eyes, pressing on his skin. Opening his mouth, he breathed deep to taste it. Something within him replied to its call, adding moss, briars and young, twining plants to the feeling in the air.

Fingers tweaked his nose. "Ow!" He rubbed the abused spot.

"Don't do that," Rosethorn said, not unkindly. "You've gotten them all excited."

"Gotten who?" He looked to see if his *shakkan* was all right. To his surprise, there were fresh green buds on some twigs. Glancing around, he saw new leaves on the plants by the windows.

"*You* know better," Rosethorn told the miniature tree. "You know very well you can't keep most of those."

"You talk like it understands," Briar complained.

Rosethorn's eyes laughed at him "It *does* understand. After a hundred and forty-six years, it knows more about how it must grow and not grow than we do."

Taking his hand, she put it on the *shakkan*'s trunk. A tickling like fire shot through him, making him wish he could roll in gravel and scratch like a dog. He yelped and pulled away. The tickling faded.

"You felt unrestrained growth, the dark side of the Green

Man," Rosethorn said. "If you let that go, the whole plant is weakened. It's in such a hurry to throw out new twigs that it doesn't take the time to build them strong. We have to cut off most of this new growth, then clip a few branches and roots. What's left will be hardier, and longer lived."

He grabbed the pot and hugged it to his chest. "You're going to *cut* it?"

The tree protested; he was bending its twigs. Briar held it away from him.

"Cutting shapes a *shakkan*. It scratches the itches. Put it on the counter."

He did as she ordered, warily.

"More than anything else, it needs a new pot. Even Crane should have seen this one is no good."

That at least made sense. "A bigger one, right?" asked Briar, scratching his itching knuckles. "That one's too small for a tree."

"No – a flatter and broader one."

Gently he touched one of the branches he'd bent, stroking the wood. "But it won't have room to grow."

"It's not *supposed* to grow, not like you mean. It's how you fit a mature tree of a century or more into a pot in the first place. Hm." She thought for a moment, arms crossed, foot tapping.

Briar put his left palm on the tree's trunk, and closed his eyes. He could feel *something* inside the living wood, like soft fire. He prodded it towards the cold spots that were the *shakkan*'s withered branches, where its fire was somehow blocked. The fire tried to obey, but the dead areas were too strong.

"I need you to go to the potters'," Rosethorn said. "And – you're sweating. Are you all right?"

Dazed, Briar let go of the *shakkan*, and wiped his forehead on his arm. "I'm fine. I was just – thinking."

"Hmpf." She looked unconvinced. Pointing to a stack of slates, and a box of white lumps beside them, she ordered, "Two slates and a piece of chalk."

Briar got them. Using the chalk, Rosethorn sketched a long rectangle, with holes at each end, then a short rectangle, both on one slate. He guessed that these were for the dish that she needed, though he couldn't read the writing she put next to each drawing.

As she wrote on the other slate, he rested his fingers on the *shakkan*'s trunk again. Before he'd itched with raw new growth. Next, he'd felt its pulse. This time he found patience, the slow and steady wait over years in sun and cloud. Eyes closed, he breathed deep of the heavy, green smell that filled the workroom once again. His nerves steadied.

"You need to keep your *shakkan* outdoors, but close to you. A shelf on your front window will do nicely." Rosethorn gave him the slates. "This one for Dedicate Watergrass at the potters', this for Dedicate Lancewood at the carpenters'. Wait for their reply, then come back. *I'm* not trimming this *shakkan* – you are."

Briar gulped, and fled.

All afternoon Sandry laboured to spin thread. Carefully she nursed her spindle, usually remembering to twirl it again before it spun in the wrong direction and undid all her work. Her attention – as much as she could spare from the spindle – was locked on her fingers as she tried to feed only small amounts of wool to the thread. There was just one more thing she wanted to do, if only to see whether she had dreamed her last days in the cellar or not.

Taking a deep breath, she tried to think only of calling light into her thread. The turning of the spindle, like a flat top at the end of a string, drew her eye, making her drowsy. She imagined threads of light pulling free of the sun's rays, coming to tangle in the wool, twisting to form a thread that was both fibre and light. Here was a glowing patch; another bit of light winked from the thread just coming from her fingers. It was time to stop and wind nearly two feet of gleaming thread on to the shaft...

When triumph at her success flooded her mind, the light in her thread flared, blinding her. The wool in her rolag, uneven in the middle, parted. The thread dropped through her fingers. Down fell the spindle, whirling counter-clockwise, undoing all her work. Every bit of light in it went dark.

Lark, who was putting a new web of thread on her floor loom, saw the girl cover her face with her hands. "You need a rest," she told Sandry. "Go outside. Look at the colours you see, and the flowers, and the people. It will go better if you relax."

"I feel so *stupid*!" Sandry collected what had once been nearly two feet of light-thread: now it was pieces of carded wool that unspun themselves where they lay. "I know *children* spin well – why can't I?"

"Perhaps children practise for longer than a week before they expect to have a proper thread," suggested Lark. "And they don't try to work magic at the same time."

"But I did the magic once before!" cried the girl.

"When you had nothing else to think about. The hammering we heard earlier didn't help *my* concentration, either. You've been at this too long, anyway. It's important to rest." Lark smiled. "Go out, Sandry. The wool can't run away."

She obeyed, walking out on to the slab of rock that served the cottage as a doorstep. Her ears rang; her muscles felt weak and unused. Glumly she looked for the source of all the hammering so close to Lark's workroom. She didn't have to look far. There was a shelf of bright, new wood on Briar's window sill.

Briar himself walked around the corner of the house, his stolen tree in his hands. Carefully, lovingly, he placed it on the shelf.

Somehow, the *shakkan* seemed different from the plant he'd stolen earlier. Curious, Sandry got to her feet. Briar flinched – he hadn't seen her there – and turned his face away when she came over to look at his prize.

"Hello," Sandry told him. The *shakkan* sported a new pot, a wide, shallow tray with a cool green finish. There were fresh cuts where branches had been nipped off and painted over with tan liquid. The twigs all looked too short, and it took a minute for her to see why: the buds had been removed.

"What did you do to it?" When he turned, she saw tear-tracks on his gold-brown cheeks. "Why are you crying?" Digging in her pocket, she produced one of her black-bordered handkerchiefs.

"I'm not crying," he growled, and swiped the back of his hand under one eye. Startled, he realized wetness was there. "Pruning hurt us," he muttered.

"Take it." Sandry thrust the handkerchief under his nose, thinking, *At least it doesn't pain me when the thread goes to pieces*. "Was it a bad hurt, like when someone kicks you, or a good one, like when a healer sets a broken bone?"

He shifted the tree slightly, wanting it to receive a perfect mix of sun and shade. "Never had a healer." He scoured his cheeks with the fine white cloth. "I guess it was a good hurt, like when I lost my baby teeth." He offered the handkerchief back to her, and saw the stains and dirt his fingers had left. "It's a mess. I'm sorry."

"Keep it," Sandry replied. "The Hataran lady who bought my mourning clothes got so many handkerchiefs, I think she expected me to cry for *years*. Can I touch the tree?"

He glanced at her, then at his *shakkan*. "Don't hurt it or scare it."

Gently, she ran a finger along the trunk. Two of the larger branches were loosely wrapped in metal spirals. "What's this wire for?"

"It helps the tree grow in the shape you want, Rosethorn said." He scuffed a bare foot – he'd misplaced his uncomfortable new shoes somewhere – on the ground. "Listen, um, thank you for – earlier." The words were hard to say. "You didn't have to do that."

"Of course I did. Maybe you'll do something for me, one day."

"Don't hold your breath," he advised, sounding more like his normal self.

She grinned at him. "Don't worry – I won't."

"Last piece of the day," Frostpine grunted, hammering a hot bar of iron. "Kirel, I need that strip *now*."

Daja watched as the apprentice put on heavy leather gloves, picked up the tongs, and drew the iron from the fire. She could see that his grip on the cherry-red metal was awkward as he turned from the forge, and nearly said so. Instead she bit her tongue. Most people Kirel's age would not like advice from an eleven-year-old girl.

The novice caught his foot, and stumbled. His tongs dropped from his grip.

She didn't think; she grabbed the hot iron before it struck the ground. Lifting it with a relieved sigh, she offered it to Kirel.

He backed up, eyes wide in horror. The forge stopped his retreat.

"Kirel? Daja?" asked Frostpine. "What's wrong?"

Daja still held the red metal out to the novice, though she had begun to shake. Just so her own kin would look at her, for handling the work of *lugsha* – for spending a whole afternoon in a *lugsha*'s shop.

Gently Frostpine reached over her shoulder and took the hot bar from her grip. Kirel ran outside.

Frostpine placed the iron on the rim of the forge. "Show me your hands."

Daja obeyed. He turned them palm up in his own – they were unmarked. "Will you get the iron from my anvil?" he asked, folding her fingers over her palms and giving them a squeeze. "Put it beside this piece – don't stick them back in the fire. Get two fresh iron bars from that box, and put them in till a third of the bar is on the coals."

"Frostpine..." she whispered, not sure of what she wanted to say.

"He'll be all right," the smith told her. "These big northern lads are just a bit high-strung." He went outside.

Daja put the iron on the fire, then stood in the doorway to cool herself off. She heard Frostpine, whispering, say, "I warned you when you came to me that you would see odd things."

"A girl who holds red-hot metal in her hands? That's more than just *odd*!"

"I don't understand why you're upset. I do the same thing, all the time."

"You're a great mage, perhaps the greatest smith-mage in the world. I always assumed you'd – you'd learned it, after years of study."

Daja stepped away, not wanting to eavesdrop any more. Once out of hearing, she regarded her hands: dark brown with tan-and-brown palms. They were striped with heavy calluses from the hard labour that went with being part of Third Ship Kisubo.

Going to the forge, she hesitated, then wrapped her hands around the red tip of the iron bar she had caught. It felt warm, but pleasantly so.

"Now," Frostpine said, coming back inside. She looked at his hands – he'd taken the hot iron from her. He wore no gloves; now that she thought of it, he hadn't worn them all afternoon. "Where were we?"

Supper was a quiet meal; only Niko, Lark and Rosethorn talked. Their four charges were exhausted after their day, half-asleep before sunset.

"We'll visit the baths now. Lark and I will clean up after we return," Rosethorn said when they had finished. "You lot go to bed early – you look done up."

"Why the change?" asked Sandry, yawning.

"Once a month we go to the Summersea market," explained Lark. "We sell goods from Winding Circle's booth."

Sandry clapped her hands; Tris sat up straight, and Daja smiled. Summersea was one of the Pebbled Sea's great ports; the market would have all sorts of interesting things.

"It's too soon for me to leave my *shakkan*," protested Briar. "I should stay with it. What if that Dedicate Crane steals it back?"

"He wouldn't dare," Rosethorn replied. "And it's no good hovering over a *shakkan*. They take their time."

Lark stood. "Everyone, collect your bathing gear. From the look of things, we'll have to make sure you don't fall asleep and drown."

The four raced to obey.

CHAPTER TEN

Up an hour before dawn the next day, they slept through most of the ride, cushioned in the cart by cloth, yarn, and bottles and crocks of liquids and ointments. By the time the sun was fully above the horizon, they were rolling through the Mire, the city's slum, part of a line of wagons, people, horses and flocks on their way to market. When they passed through the city wall between the Mire and Summersea proper, Briar sighed with relief. He was not sure how he felt, looking at a slum that was so much like the one where he grew up.

The immense market square was jammed with merchants and shoppers. Once they reached her booth, Rosethorn wasted no time in putting everyone to work setting their wares on the shelves and table. Once the cart was empty but for a canvas-wrapped bolt of cloth, Lark drove off. Niko, who had accompanied them on horseback, followed her.

Briar and Daja – who had brought her staff – guarded the booth. Sandry and Tris showed goods, looked up prices, and wrapped the items that were sold. Rosethorn talked to favoured customers while handling the cash box. It was a busy morning, with hardly a moment of quiet. All of them ate their midday standing up.

Soon after that, Lark returned. "We can let them go, can't we, Rosie? You and I can mind things."

Rosethorn eyed their charges. "Promise to stay together? And out of trouble?"

"We promise," they chorused.

She pointed to the Guildhall clock. "Return by three." Taking coins from her belt-purse, she handed them out. "Here's five copper crescents each. Don't buy anything illegal. Now, scat!"

"Come *on*," Briar said when Sandry hesitated.

"Before she changes her mind," Daja added. She grabbed one of Sandry's arms, Briar the other, and they dragged her away. Tris brought up the rear.

Their first stop was a sweet shop, where they spent a crescent apiece; their second was at the market fountain, to wash their sticky hands. After that they wandered among the stalls. Sandry found a wooden drop spindle painted dark green, and bought it. Tris located a seller of used books and dived into his crates, examining each volume. The others drifted away. Finding a copper-monger's stall on the outer rim of the square, Daja stopped to admire his finely worked serving dishes. Briar struck up a conversation with two ragged boys.

Finding a spot where people wouldn't bump her, Sandry eyed the buildings around the square nearby: Summersea Guildhall, Provost's Hall, Traders' Hall. The Guildhall in particular was very fine, with statues of craftsmen tucked in niches around the first storey. She was about to go and have a closer look when a dog's yelp, followed by human laughter, got her attention. Looking around, she saw an alley where six boys, fairly well-dressed, were bent over something.

"Stop that!" she cried. Running over, she seized a boy. "How dare you!"

Her captive – a big youth in a green tunic – slammed her, knocking her on to a pile of rubbish. Scrambling to her feet, Sandry hit another lad. He tried to kick her, but managed somehow to tangle his foot in her skirt. Grabbing his ankle, she twisted, dumping him on to his back. She seized his neighbour, trying to drag him away from the others. That boy caught one of her braids, and yanked hard. With a scream that was as much rage as pain, Sandry bit his arm. He yelled, and punched her in the stomach.

Hearing a commotion, Daja looked around. Briar was still talking to the ragged boys; Tris was bargaining for a book. Where was Sandry?

"Bullies!" she heard a familiar voice cry. "Oafs! Torturing an animal..."

"Get out of here!" yelled someone at the square's edge. A small figure went flying away from a group of boys, to hit a wall.

Daja gripped her staff tightly and ran to Sandry's aid.

The boy who had thrown Sandry against the wall wasn't done with her. As he raised a fist, something hard walloped him across the shoulders. He spun around to face a black girl nearly his own height, equipped with a Trader's staff.

He swung at her. From the ground, Sandry kicked at the backs of his knees; Daja rammed the head of the staff into his midriff. He went down hard, rolling into a clump of horse manure.

"Behind you!" Sandry cried to her friend.

Daja thanked the luck-gods that her uncles had insisted she learn a few staff tricks very well. Putting the weapon between arm and side, she drove the smooth wood into the air behind her until it hit someone hard. He yelped. She turned, and banged him on the side of the neck, making him retreat. Three more town boys waded in.

"Ho, it's a tumble," one of Briar's new acquaintances remarked. "Town girls, too. Not bad, for town girls."

"Th' one's Trader," noted the other street rat. "Trader staff, anyways."

Briar turned to look; the "town" girl was Sandry. What was he supposed to do, rescue her and Daja? Because they lived together, did that make them his gang?

He sighed. He *did* owe Sandry for yesterday, and in Deadman's District, debts always had to be paid sooner than later.

Besides, it looked like a good fight, against plump merchant boys. With a nod to the street rats, he ran to help the girls.

He took the enemy by surprise, kicking Green Tunic between the legs from behind. As another boy swung on him, Briar ducked. Gripping the enemy's arm, he twisted it up behind him, and shoved him into a boy who was trying to rise from a manure pile.

Daja whacked a boy with her staff. Sandry, on the ground, yanked at the breeches of a boy who waited to get at Briar, pulling them around his knees. When he stumbled and fell, she wriggled by. There, at the mouth of the alley, was the shivering, blood-streaked ball of fur that had cried in pain. Grabbing the puppy, she hugged it to her.

"Town-lads!" cried Green Tunic, who seemed to be the leader. "Town-lads, to me!"

"None of that!" Briar rammed him in the stomach, knocking the air from the larger boy's lungs. "You do your *own* fighting!"

At the bookseller's, Tris tucked her purchase into a pocket and looked for the others. When she spotted them, she began to tremble. Fights meant pain and getting in trouble. She *hated* getting hurt.

Daja was in the thick of it, laying about her with her

staff like a woman beating carpets she didn't like. Briar darted from one enemy to the next, doing quick things that made them bellow and curse. There was Sandry, lobbing a brown mass that she'd scooped from the gutter into one boy's face.

More youths ran by, intent on the fight. They outnumbered Tris's housemates, and most of them were bigger, as well. She suddenly had an image of the embroidered wall hanging that Sandry had given her so casually. It was a beautiful thing. In twilight, she'd found, the needlework birds almost seemed alive.

If she helped, the boys would hurt her; *that* had happened to her before. Frantic, she looked around for a constable or any other adult who might break things up. Instead, the alley where the fight was drew her eyes. At its far end she could see the blue-grey waters of Summersea harbour.

She wasn't sure what happened next. Her mind broke free of panic, like a kite that had just caught the wind. Air bore her up, as it had the first time that she had tried meditation, and carried her to the harbour. Drawing her mind close, concentrating on a small patch of water, she drew it up with an invisible bucket. She would bring it to the town boys, to cool them off.

A rude hand grabbed her shoulder and whipped her around, breaking her concentration. "Out of my way!" snapped a youth as he shoved her aside.

Confused, Tris shook her head, and turned until she could see harbour and alley again. On the docks, in full view, a waterspout – a water cyclone – twirled like a very thin top. The boy had spun *her*, and she had spun her seawater. "Uh-oh," she whispered.

When it was ten feet tall, the waterspout jumped free of the dock. Wobbling, it advanced down the alley, pulling crates, garbage and gutter-muck into itself as it came.

"Excuse me?" Tris ran toward the fight. "I think you should stop..."

No one heard. The waterspout caught up with a pair of boys. Grabbing them, it spat them against the alley walls. A third boy turned, and was seized head-first. He rose nearly seven feet before the spout dumped him.

Daja, Briar and Sandry couldn't see the alley – they were around the corner, in the main square. There a youth raised his hands to block Daja's staff; she switched its angle, and knocked his feet from under him. Briar twisted a boy's nose, then fell back until he and Daja guarded Sandry and the pup. Carefully, the three of them retreated. Three town youths followed.

A watery cyclone sprang from the alley. The town boys, not knowing what came at them from the rear, saw shock in their foe's eyes. "That's the oldest trick there is!" Green Tunic jeered. He sported the beginnings of a black eye. His partner, with two swollen lips, laughed harshly. Only the third youth turned to look – then ran. The spout gulped the other two, spun them rapidly a few times, then spat them on to the cobbles of the square.

Watching all this, Tris shook with terror. She was in *real* trouble this time. This was no bolt of lightning, to strike and vanish. Already it had pummelled some boys; now it advanced on her housemates. She ought to start running, and not stop until she reached Namorn.

The puppy escaped Sandry's hold, and ran at the water-spout, yapping and snarling. Sandry dived for him, and mis-sed.

Until now, Tris's only friends were animals. "No, no!"

Running up, she thrust herself in front of her creation, before it could seize the dog. "Stop right now! I – I command it! Please?"

The spout halted, pulling in on itself. Tris stared at it, forbidding it to move. Sweat rolled down her cheeks and back. Now what could she do?

The spout shifted to her right. The moment she saw the scoured-white cobbles where it had been she said grimly, "Oh, no, you *don't.*" Inhaling, she reached towards her creation with her mind. She instantly felt invisible ties that stretched between her and this water-and-garbage monster. Wrapping her mind around them, Tris gripped them hard, like reins, and tugged the waterspout, until it returned to its original position.

"I'll get Lark or Rosethorn." Daja thrust her staff into Briar's hands. "Here – in case someone else gets ideas." She backed up, then ran around the waterspout, giving it a wide berth. Its upper half bent out of line, trying to follow her.

"Stop it!" cried Tris. This was starting to *hurt*; she could feel needles of pain in her head and neck. What would happen when she lost control?

Sandry drew close. Scooping up the dog, she wrapped her free, mucky hand around Tris's. Briar gripped the redhead's shoulder. Tris felt the stronger for their nearness. Taking a breath, she let it out, and forbade the waterspout to go *anywhere*.

It shrank, then lengthened, fighting. Tris held firm. The spout whirled faster – then spat out the trash that it had collected in the alley. A slab of wood banged Tris on the forehead. She yowled, and clapped a hand to the gash, feeling blood spill over her fingers. Briar and Sandry braced her.

"You gotta hold it!" Briar cried as the spout muttered to

itself. "C'mon, merchant-girl, this's no time to worry about an ouch!"

Hissing, the spout tore at the cobbles, throwing rock splinters into the air. Tris's hold on it broke as all three of them covered their eyes. With a roar of triumph, the waterspout turned on the market.

"Enough," a familiar voice said. Daja, Lark and Rosethorn had arrived to block the spout's path. Lark held up a drop spindle, one that already carried blue yarn. Her fingers twisted; the spindle whirled left, against the proper twist. She let it slip down, her eyes fixed on the waterspout as the thread opened up. The water cyclone's motion slowed, then reversed. It stretched, and stretched, and collapsed, dropping into a puddle that washed away from Lark. Halting the spindle, Lark wound her unspun wool around one hand.

With the fall of her creation, Tris felt the ground lurch. Her bones felt like water, trickling into her shoes. She sagged, and Briar caught her.

Rosethorn glared at them. "You were told to stay out of trouble."

"It wasn't so bad." Briar put a hand over an eye that was rapidly going black. "Nobody was killed."

"They were torturing this dog!" Sandry was still red with fury. "It's just a puppy, and they were hurting it!"

"Come on." Rosethorn grabbed Daja and Sandry, and headed back into the market, towing them with her. Lark and Briar supported the wobbly Tris. "If we hurry," Rosethorn explained, "we might get out of the city with no one the wiser."

The cart, with the placid cob that drew it, stood beside the booth. "I can't believe no one nicked it," Briar said, awed.

"Never mind that. Start packing," Rosethorn ordered.

Lark and Briar put Tris in the cart first, then their things. That was a fast job – almost everything had been sold. The other children clambered into the cart after that. Daja, holding the dog as Sandry got settled, heard a roar, and looked around. A crowd was approaching. "Rosethorn – trouble."

Both dedicates turned, and saw what she meant. "So much for leaving before someone makes a fuss," Lark murmured.

"You'll answer for what you've done!" cried a wealthy-looking man.

A woman called, "You half-killed my boy!"

Sandry rose, twitching her skirt away as Briar tried to pull her back down. "Your *boy* hurt a helpless animal!" she cried, eyes blazing. "Shame on him!"

"Shut up," Rosethorn said out of the corner of her mouth.

"The square's tore apart. Who's to pay for that?" The speaker, a man in the knee-length tunic worn by Hatarans, halted before them. "And there's penalty taxes for brawling in the marketplace."

"There was no warning posted for a big magical working!" A woman drew close, a battered Green Tunic under her arm. "Plus there's healer's fees for my son. A fine thing, when children can't play while their folks are at market!"

"He deserved a worse thrashing than he got!" Sandry snatched the puppy from Daja and held it up. "*Here's* what he and his friends were *playing* at. I'd be ashamed to own up to such a son!"

Now both Daja and Briar were trying to make her sit.

Sandry yanked free. "Only a brute has fun by hurting animals! To—"

"Shut up, Sandry, *please*!" Everyone stared at the cart, startled by the agonized cry. Tris fought to sit up. Her voice as harsh as a raven's, she croaked, "Isn't it bad enough? Leave it!"

The pup whimpered, and thrust his nose into the crook of Sandry's arm. With a sigh, the girl sat down. "But only for *you*," she murmured to him. Digging a handkerchief from her pocket, she tried to clean his bleeding cuts.

"Maybe we need a truthsayer," Rosethorn suggested. "Question the boys *and* our charges, to get the whole story."

"I'm sure Master Niko would act as truthsayer." Two men rode out of a lane between stalls, followed by soldiers in the brown leather jerkins, blue shirts and breeches of the Provost's guard. "That *is* part of your skills, isn't it, Niko?" Duke Vedris asked his companion. The Duke was simply dressed in a plain wine-red shirt, leather breeches and a leather jerkin studded with metal rings. A heavy gold ring gleamed in one of his ears.

All around them, adults and children bowed deep, saying, "Your Grace."

Briar looked at Daja, then Sandry. "Who's the Bag?"

"Duke Vedris," Sandry replied, as Daja glanced at her, startled. "The ruler of Emelan."

"I often work as a truthsayer, your Grace," Niko told the Duke. "If it will simplify things, I can do so here." He rode over until he could lean down and press a hand briefly to Tris's cheek. She grabbed his fingers and hung on.

"Your Grace," cried Green Tunic's mother, "my boy was attacked with *magic*! Look at him!"

"Look at *our* sons," someone else shouted. "They too were attacked!"

"One of them called up a waterspout," said a wealthy-looking man in the leggings and long coat-tunic of the Traders. "What if it had turned on ships? It nearly struck the market. You can see where it dug cobbles from the street."

Sandry passed the dog to Briar, and stood with hands folded neatly in front of her. "Your Grace, may I have leave to speak?" Her voice, polite and clear, rang through the air. If no one could have seen her torn and muddied clothes, they might have thought she was a queen in her throne room. "It is my right."

The Duke leaned on his saddle-horn. "As one accused, you may speak, Lady Sandrilene fa Toren." His voice was soft, but clear. "Proceed."

"A *noble*?" asked someone, clearly surprised.

"You never said she was a lady," Green Tunic's mother accused.

"She *bit* me, Ma! And she's dressed like normal folk!"

Sandry waited until everyone was quiet. "Your Grace, my friends and I were visiting the market when I heard an animal cry." Her small face was pale and set; she kept her chin up. "Six boys were hurting it, in an alley back there." She pointed. "If you assign blame for the fight, give it to me, please. *I* attacked them. My friends came to help *me* – just as the boys' friends came to help *them*. And I still think they were very, very wrong to harm a helpless animal."

"Did you inflict *all* of these injuries, Lady Sandrilene?" Her uncle's voice was stern, but the corner of his mouth quivered.

Daja rose, leaning on her staff. "Some of that was me, your grace."

The Trader who had spoken glanced at her. "*Trangshi*," he muttered. Sandry glared at him. He met her furious eyes once, then looked away.

Ashamed, Daja bit the inside of her cheek, then went on.

"San – Lady Sandry is *saati* – a true friend. They knocked her down, and I went after them."

"Don't be greedy," said Briar, getting to his feet. He passed the dog to Sandry. "Some of these poor sniffers' ouches are mine, your worship, sir."

"But this is a quarrel of children," objected the Duke, looking with confusion at the townspeople.

"There was magic!" cried the Trader. "A waterspout attacked the boys!"

"It was an accident!" Tris lurched to her feet. "I meant to dump water on them, and only water!" She broke off, crimson, then swallowed, and went on. "I lifted it out of the sea, and – somebody spun me around." She wiped her sweaty face on a sleeve. "When I looked again, the water was *spinning*. I couldn't – it got away from me!"

The Duke straightened, his eyes now cold. The chatter going on under the main discussion stopped. Everyone watched Vedris IV.

"Two cases are before me," he said in that clear, quiet voice. "In the matter of injuries done to these youths, the healers' bills shall come to me, to be paid by funds held in trust for these young people. *But* – those bills must be for legitimate wounds, and they must be sworn to before a truthsayer."

"That'll stop the fakers," Briar muttered in Daja's ear. She nodded.

The Duke folded his hands on his saddle-horn. "There is also the matter of cruelty to an animal." Daja and Briar saw people's eyes widen. "The law is plain. Here in Emelan, where the Living Circle is honoured" – he nodded to Lark and Rosethorn, who bowed – "we no more harm animals for sport than we do human beings. The fine, for those who have forgotten, is twenty silver astrels.

"Those who wish repayment for the healer's fees will tell the truthsayers if they are also liable for damage to the animal. If they are, the fine for *that* must be paid first. All parties will pay the truthsayer's fee."

For a moment no one made a sound. Twenty silver astrels was three months' income for a poor man, a month's income for a craftsman. Truthsayers were even more expensive than the fine.

The woman who had been eager to proclaim Green Tunic's innocence was the first to reply. "We need no truthsayer or healer," she told the Duke, bobbing a curtsey. She gripped her son by one ear, and dragged him away. Other youths and their families thought the better of involving truthsayers, and left as well.

To those who remained – some merchants, a handful of Traders, and the group from Winding Circle – the Duke said, "Penalties for the unlicensed use of magic are high. This must also be addressed." Heads nodded everywhere.

"Your Grace, if I may," Niko said. "Trisana did not know she is a mage. The law *does* make allowance for the – accidents – caused by young mages, without proper teaching."

"Poppycock!" yelled a baker in a floury apron. "How could she not know? This was a ship-killer, not milk curdling in the churn!"

"If she's ignorant of it, why is she with Lark and Rosethorn?" a woman snapped. "Everyone knows the mageborn are placed in their care!"

Briar, Sandry and Daja looked at each other, startled.

"So that's why nobody nicked the cart and horse," Briar muttered.

"My kinfolk told me I was crazy!" Tris cried, her voice

cracking. "The tester said I had no magic, and they got rid of me!"

Lark climbed into the back of the wagon and drew Tris close. "She's exhausted," Lark told the Duke. "She needs food, and she needs to go to bed. If you mean to punish her, may we wait until she knows what's happening?"

People left, shaking their heads. A sick girl wasn't nearly as worrisome as a mage who deliberately used her magic for harm.

"Are you satisfied?" the Duke asked the three who stayed: the baker, a man with a goldsmith's badge on his hat, and the Trader who had called Daja *trangshi.*

"Until we hear of another such incident," said the goldsmith. "She's a danger to everyone as she is."

"And if I confine her to Winding Circle until Master Niko says that she has control over her power?" the Duke wanted to know. "Is that agreeable?"

"If they return to Winding Circle as soon as possible, I will be satisfied," replied the baker. The goldsmith nodded.

The Trader said nothing, only turned and walked away. Daja watched him go, her hand tightening on her staff until her knuckles were white.

The Duke looked the children over. "What of that animal?" he asked Sandry.

Rosethorn started to protest, then sighed. "The dog stays with us," she said.

"There, you heard that?" Sandry asked her new friend. "You belong to us now." The pup whimpered, and licked her face.

Instead of leaving the city immediately and getting caught in the after-market jam of horses and carts, they accepted the Duke's offer of supper at a nearby eating-house and a guard to accompany them home. Through the meal, Lark concentrated on Tris, cajoling and bullying the exhausted girl into eating.

Once their bellies were full, the other three were allowed to bathe their new pet in the tiny yard behind the eating-house. Rosethorn anointed his cuts with a sharp-smelling balm. "You four get to train this fierce, wolf-like creature to take his business out of doors," she told them as she worked. "*And* clean up after him, and stop him from chewing everything in sight." When the dog snapped at her touch on a particularly ugly wound, she gripped him gently by the muzzle. "Enough," she said. "I don't like dogs any more than I like children."

Sheepish, the pup wagged his tail, and whined at her. He didn't snap again.

As Sandry and Daja took the cleaned-up dog out to show Niko, Lark and the Duke, Briar helped Rosethorn to gather her medicines. "I'm no mage," he said abruptly.

"Nonsense," was the tart reply. "You're as much a mage as I am. It's just that your magic – the girls' too, if it comes to that – shows itself in unusual ways."

He put a hand on her arm. "Niko has it wrong. *I'm no mage.*"

Rosethorn looked meaningfully at the hand on her sleeve, until he withdrew it, a blush staining his gold-brown cheeks. "It's no accident that Niko was at your sentencing – he'd had a premonition of a boy with the green magic in him. I knew he was right when I heard my bean plants welcome you. You got them all excited, my buck. They wanted to throw out seed pods a month early. I had to be stern with them."

"That ain't magic," he protested.

"Of course it is, and important magic at that. The most

important, to my way of thinking. You don't need to share that with Lark or Niko."

"I'm a thief," he protested.

"I bet you had a lot of plants like moss and mushrooms in whatever hole you lived in," she said, dark eyes sharp. "I bet strange things happened to you in rich men's gardens."

The boy hung his head, rubbing a thumb over the deep scars in his palm. Rosethorn touched the hand. Her fingertips found each large, dimpled pock left by the vine whose name he had taken.

"They grow big-thorned briars to protect the tops of garden walls," she remarked. "This one must have *loved* you, to leave so deep a scar."

"With mates like that plant, I don't need constables," he mumbled. Something cool poured into the old wounds and up his arm. Scented with turning leaves and wet stone, it was the thing he'd smelled in her shop, the day they'd worked on the *shakkan*. Looking into her face, he saw the glint of green and gold in her eyes, and felt the pull of life that flowed through her stocky frame: the kind of power that could sink tendrils into rock and split it open, given time.

"Magic?" he whispered.

"Go tell Niko it's time to leave," she ordered. "We need to be home before the Earth temple's midnight worship."

Once they returned to the cart, Tris was bundled up in blankets fetched from the guards' barracks. She went to sleep almost immediately. The other three made themselves comfortable among the empty sacks, as Rosethorn took the reins. Lark rode double with Niko for the moment, behind the cart; they were talking quietly. The Duke and his soldiers came as well, the squad breaking in two so that five guards marched ahead of the cart, five behind. The Duke rode beside the cart, talking to Rosethorn about the summer crops.

Sandry put the pup down, smiling as he tried to steady himself against the cart's lurch. Clumsily he tottered over to each of them, even the sleeping Tris, and gave them a good sniff.

"He probably has fleas," Briar remarked. The pup wagged his tail.

"He likes you," said Daja tiredly. "No accounting for taste."

"Can we call him Little Bear?" asked Sandry. "He looks like a bear, when he's standing. His feet stick out in that flat bear way."

"Enough of this *we*," snapped Briar tiredly. "Just because we had a tumble, it don't turn us into mates. What happened back there don't mean a thing!"

"Touchy!" retorted Daja, throwing up her hands. "I'm sorry they've got us in the same cart!"

Sandry put a hand on her arm. "It's too hot to fight, Daja."

The puppy whined at Briar.

"You don't know these girls yet," Briar told him. "They'd drive a tortoise to a frenzy."

"Did you know?" Sandry asked. "About – magic?"

He went still, staring at her. After a moment, he looked away. "No," he whispered.

Sandry tugged first on her left braid, then on her right. "I sort of did, back in Hatar, after my parents died." Quietly she told them about the hidden room, back when smallpox had ravaged all Hatar, and a mob had killed the only person who knew where she was. "I didn't think the light was real, for a long time," she told them. "It's only been in the last two days that I thought maybe I was wrong."

"We aren't allowed to talk to *lugsha* – people who make things," Daja replied softly. "I was kept away from smiths. I never guessed – Kirel acted so odd..."

"You aren't making a word of sense," Briar growled.

Daja took a deep breath, and explained what had taken place when Frostpine's apprentice dropped a piece of red-hot iron. She looked at her hands. "It felt like my friend. And Kirel was scared of me."

Briar whistled softly. "What about the redhead?" he asked, pointing at Tris.

"The redhead will keep her sad story to herself," replied Tris coldly, without opening her eyes. "And she'll be very happy if you keep your 'neb' out of her business!" Rolling over, she turned her back to them.

"Sweet as ever," muttered Briar. He tugged a few empty sacks around to make a nest for himself, curled up, and closed his eyes.

In Tradertalk Daja murmured, "I told you," to Sandry. "She's plain mean."

The other girl shook her head. Tris could growl and snap all she liked. During their brawl, when the waterspout had tried to attack Daja, Tris had clearly been terrified – and had dealt with her creation in spite of her fear, to keep it from hurting the Trader. To Sandry, that act counted more than anything that a worn-out Tris might say.

At the city gates, Lark climbed into the back of the cart with the children, and settled herself for a nap. The squad of soldiers from the Provost guard, whose authority ended at the city wall, was replaced by a squad of the Duke's guard. They and the Duke accompanied the cart through the Mire and its resident criminals, and up the long road to Winding Circle. By then Briar and Daja were asleep, as Tris pretended to be. Sandry climbed up to sit beside Rosethorn, so she could admire the view of the harbour islands lit by the two great lighthouses that guarded Summersea's port.

Once they were well past the Mire, the Duke got Rosethorn's attention. "May I drive for a time?" he asked. "Even if you are not accustomed to riding, you will find Ladylove a comfortable mount."

Briar opened a sleepy eye when Rosethorn laughed, and accepted the offer. As calmly as if he drove carts for a living, the duke settled into her place and took up the reins.

"I hope I didn't put you on the spot back in the market," Sandry remarked quietly. "I didn't think you would favour me just because you're my great-uncle."

Unnoticed by Sandry or the Duke, Briar sat up, furious. Her uncle! Wasn't that a Bag for you? Of course she could be brave about standing up for them – she must have known he wouldn't punish her!

"Nor did I favour you." The Duke put his arm around Sandry. "I would have delivered the same judgement had total strangers been involved." If he heard Briar's unbelieving snort, he ignored it. "I *would* like to say now that your father and mother would have been proud of you."

She ducked her head, glad that the darkness hid her blush. "Truly?"

"I do. *I* am proud of you in their place."

For a moment they listened to the footsteps of horses and soldiers, and the distant boom of the sea. When Vedris took his arm away, Sandry asked, "Did you know, Uncle? About the magic?"

For a moment she thought he would not answer. Then she heard his velvet-soft voice: "Your parents lived in such an *odd* way. I must believe it never occurred to them that new oddities might have their child at the source. Your own life with them was one oddity after another – what did you have to compare it to?"

She yawned. "It complicates things, doesn't it?"

Though it was too dark to see his face, she heard a smile in his voice. "My dear Sandrilene, you have a talent for—"

"I'm going to be sick," Tris interrupted, voice high. She lurched to her feet, gripping the sides of the cart. Briar steadied her. "I..."

"Tris?" Niko urged his mount over to her. "What is it?"

"A wave – there's a wave in the ground!" she gasped, eyes wide. "Tide's coming in!"

"Impossible." The Duke halted the cart. "My dear, you are dreaming..."

"I feel dizzy," Sandry whispered. The pup whined, and barked frantically. Daja awoke. The cart was shivering.

Lark sat up, pushing her hair out of her eyes. "Are we on a boat?" asked the dedicate sleepily.

The guards before and behind them lurched, barely keeping on their feet. A handful of small rocks tumbled across the road as it shuddered, and went still.

"Earthquake summer," whispered a soldier.

"No earthquakes for me." Tris wiped her sweaty face on her sleeve. "I've had enough fun so far, thanks all the same."

Briar released her as some of the guards laughed nervously.

"You feel any more such waves coming, missy, you let us know," their sergeant directed Tris. "We'll appreciate it."

Once they reached Winding Circle, they parted company with the Duke and his guardsmen. Seeing that Niko was about to ride on, to help Lark as she took cart and mule back to the temple stables, Tris muttered, "I wish we could talk to him."

Sandry heard. "Niko?" she called. "Might we – the four of us and you – have a word?"

"Can't it wait until tomorrow?" he asked.

"Now is better," said Daja firmly.

"Time to face the music," Lark told Niko with a grin. He shrugged and dismounted. "I believe I'll take your horse to the stables," volunteered Rosethorn. "Since you're staying here with the kids."

"Coward," Niko told her. He walked into the cottage, and the children followed, Little Bear trotting from the centre of their group.

Inside, he called up magical light to fill the main room. "You have something to say to me?" he asked, sitting on a chair.

"Why didn't you tell us?" Tris's voice was harsh with tiredness and emotion. "If you'd even *hinted*—"

"You, my dear, were adamant that you had no magic. I think that it was the only way that you could bear your family turning you out, if you thought there was something dreadful and alien that was wrong with you." In the even glow of his light, Niko's eyes were like black gems. "I feared that if you learned the truth too soon you would reject it, and keep rejecting it."

"What about me?" Daja asked. "And Sandry, and Briar? Nobody told us, either."

Niko sighed. "All four of you have endured a very difficult year, in one way or another. My reasoning was the same as it was for Tris: I preferred that you *grow* into knowing your power, instead of having it thrust on you, to keep from damaging your spirits any more than they've been. Were you all that surprised to hear it today?"

"Yes," growled Briar.

Daja looked at her hands again, and remembered Kirel telling Frostpine, "*You're a great mage, perhaps the greatest smith-mage in the world.*" "Why didn't our people know?" she asked. "Why didn't the *mimanders* pick me out?"

"Why didn't that magic-tester know?" asked Tris. She sank to the floor and gathered the puppy into her lap. "He was supposed to be the best in all Capchen."

"I think I understand a little. We don't do things like normal mages, do we?" Sandry enquired. "None of us made our toys move when we were small, I bet. Or made pictures for people to see in a fire, or made things glow?" She looked at the others as she said it, trying to see the answers in their faces. "Those are the usual mageborn things. I never did any of them."

Briar shook his head.

"We're tested for it when we turn four," murmured Daja. "They found no magic in me."

"It isn't their fault," Niko said crisply. "Even I had to look very deeply to see the power that's in each of you, and my *speciality* is finding things – and people – that are hidden. That's why I brought you here, instead of to the university. There are more mages in Winding Circle whose power speaks through workaday things, plain things, as yours does."

"So our power isn't that big or important," grumbled Tris.

Niko sighed. "It is greater than you think. There is weather, or threadcraft" – he pointed to Sandry – "or metalwork, or growing plants" – he pointed to Daja and Briar in turn – "everywhere in the world. People cannot live without any of these things. They may not like it, but they *can* live without the products of traditional magery, such as love potions and seeing the future."

"Kirel said Frostpine might be the greatest smith-mage in the world," Daja said. "That sounds important to *me*."

"It is – and Frostpine has searched for twenty long years for a student who shares his gift," replied Niko. "Any more questions?"

The four were silent. The long day had caught up with them all, and suddenly no magic in the world seemed as good to them as their own beds.

"Then I will see you in the morning." Niko levered himself to his feet. "It's time for you to get to work, now that you *know* what we're dealing with."

CHAPTER ELEVEN

The next day Discipline's residents grumpily returned to their schedule. All of the humans felt the lack of sleep and the over-excitement from the day before. Only Little Bear, making himself at home – and learning that certain important dog acts were not to be done inside Discipline – was lively that morning.

For Daja the hours until afternoon crawled. She rushed through the dishes, even helping Briar to dry them in her hurry. When Sandry asked Niko why Lark and Rosethorn once again walked a thread-and-herb circle around the cottage, Daja thought she would scream with frustration; she just wanted to get meditation over with. She fidgeted as Niko explained that the circles were only needed until the four mastered the mind-gathering-in exercise. Once they were able to keep their undisciplined power from spilling all over Winding Circle, there would be no more need for magic to contain them as they meditated.

Tris gasped. "You mean 'Discipline' – this house – doesn't mean punishment?"

"Well, it can be taken as punishment," said Niko, with an eye on the restless Daja. "But more importantly, discipline is what you are here to learn."

That Daja heard. "Sorry," she mumbled, dark cheeks going red with shame. She did try harder to calm down after that.

Finally the Hub clock sounded the end of the rest period. Daja nearly flew down the road to the smithies. Breathless and drawn by the music of hammering, she walked into Frostpine's iron forge. Kirel, at work shaping a red-hot strip of metal, nodded.

Frostpine waved the girl over to where he lounged against the long counter. "I understand you had a lively day at the market," he remarked with a smile.

"Why didn't you tell me?" she asked, panting. "You knew I have magic."

He smoothed his beard with a broad hand. "Learning to work metal is more important," he said flatly. When Daja blinked at him, not understanding, the smith began to pace. "This – odd power that I have, that you have, it's not like that of university mages. They draw a design on the ground, mumble a few words, and get results. Not us. Our magic only works as well as the things it passes through. If you can't bring a forge-fire to white heat with a bellows, or work an iron bar so that it won't break on impact, or melt down ores without removing the dross..." He shrugged. "The magic is only as strong as your fire or metal. It's only as pure as the ore you melt down. Before you become a mage, you must be a smith. You must work metal and magic together."

He stopped, and blinked. "I made a speech, didn't I?"

For a moment, she didn't understand what he'd said last. His words had sounded a note so deep inside Daja that her bones still rang with it.

Frostpine cupped her face in his hands. "Daja?"

She took a deep breath. "I want to learn. I want to learn *everything*."

He smiled at her. "I knew that." Releasing her, he pointed at the counter. On it was placed a line of cloth-covered lumps. "Come tell me what these are." When she reached for a cloth, he stopped her. "*Before* you look."

"You mean with magic."

"Use anything except sight. These are common metals, ones you've seen and handled in some form. It should be easy." He drew his hand away.

Daja stepped up to the counter. What was she supposed to do? Nervously, one eye on Frostpine in case he objected, she put her left hand on the first lump, and took a deep breath – then another – then a third.

Did it have a smell? Bending, she sniffed the air over the cloth. The scent was barely present, an acid sharpness. Carefully she rubbed her fingers over the lump, and inhaled that tang again. What was that county, in the southwest? They had dropped anchor for two scant days, before her mother decided that there were too many warring tribes for safe trading. She couldn't remember the name, but she had helped to log the copper jewellery they got in those two days.

"Copper?" she asked Frostpine.

"That doesn't sound like you're sure."

It had been her first landfall with the ship, and the jewellery was beautiful. Her mother had worn a brooch from that cargo until the ship went down.

"I'm sure," she told him.

Frostpine lifted off the cloth. "Very good," he said, as Daja touched the blobby piece of raw copper. "Next." He pointed to the second lump.

She touched it, and knew right away, though she couldn't say how. "Gold."

He uncovered three small nuggets. "Not surprising, after you drew gold wire."

Daja picked the nuggets up. They almost sang against her

fingers, as if she clutched sunlight. Smiling, she put them down.

Frostpine pointed to the next lump. "And...?"

She smelled the air over it; she pressed her fingers all over the cloth. She knew it, but not by itself. "I give up," she said at last. "It makes me crazy, because I *ought* to know, and I don't."

"Perhaps you're getting tired," suggested Frostpine. "Try that one. If it doesn't work, you can rest."

She placed a limp hand on the cloth, feeling like a dolt. She *ought* to know what each and every thing he showed her was. She ought to!

Forcing those thoughts from her mind, she concentrated on the thing under her hand. It was worked metal: she knew that from the shape, smooth and slightly curved. Her fingers detected bumps that formed a design.

Of *course* she knew it! She'd handled and stowed plenty of bronze aboard ship. It was marvellous stuff. This bit in particular seemed to hang, glowing, in her mind. Absorbed, she closed her eyes, exploring it with her thoughts. Part of bronze was copper – not only had she learned that years ago, but now she *felt* the copper in this piece. Moreover, the rest, that part which wasn't copper, was – tin. In trading classes, she'd learned that bronze was a mix of copper and tin.

She'd felt tin recently.

Daja jerked the cloth off the metal she couldn't identify before. A small pile of heavy black lumps met her eyes. "It's *tin*," she told Frostpine, gleeful. "Because it's copper and tin that make bronze!"

Frostpine grinned. "Daja, we are going to have *fun* together," he promised.

"Can I play, too?" asked a forlorn voice. Unnoticed by

them, Kirel had finished the piece he worked on, and had come over to watch. He smiled ruefully at his master and at Daja. "I'll be good."

That evening, after supper and baths, the residents of Discipline made themselves comfortable in the main room. Little Bear, his belly round with the meal of scraps he had gulped, sprawled on the floor and slept, paws twitching as he dreamed. Bringing her new spindle and the rolags she had prepared that afternoon, Sandry took a chair beside Lark, who did her own spinning while helping the girl with hers. Briar had four plants which he had yanked from the ground by mistake, thinking they were weeds. Rosethorn ordered him to memorize them by sight and scent, and *never* pluck them again. She herself sat at the table, writing in a ledger. Niko sat next to her, writing letters.

Like Briar, Daja had memorizing to do. Frostpine had given her drawings of several types of hammer, each with a written description of its use, to learn within the week. Tris had a library book, one that described the early lives of five great mages.

For a while the only indoor sounds were the scratch of pens, the rustle of paper, and Sandry's mutterings when thread unwound, or a rolag came apart. More noise drifted through open doors and windows: the soft chime as the Hub clock sounded every fifteen minutes, or its deeper tones as it called the hour, the muted laughter and clatter as people went by on the spiral road, the night-songs of crickets and peepers.

With nearly three feet of freshly-spun thread – lumpy, too thick in some places and too thin in others – wound on her spindle, Sandry took a break. Rolling her head on her neck, as she often saw Lark do, she got up and walked around. Returning from a look outside, she discovered that Briar was toying with some stray pieces of wool. He twisted it in his fingers.

"What are you doing?" she asked as he added another tuft of wool to his string. "*Your* magic's with plants." If he didn't hold down the piece he'd already twirled, it did not just unwind – it sprang apart. When he reached for the tufts he'd collected from her earlier mistakes, they puffed into balls or blew out of his fingers.

"But that spinning looks interesting," he replied, grabbing more bits of wool. "Relaxing, like."

Rosethorn looked up from her ledger. "Learning to spin isn't a bad idea," she commented thoughtfully. "We need a lot of string for our work. Forget wool and silk, though. Those are from sheep, or little worms. People like us are better off with cotton and flax." Rosethorn grinned. "They come from plants."

"Sandry, will you teach me?" asked the boy, still trying to get his tufts under control. "If I can find this other stuff to spin?"

"I'm only learning myself," she pointed out. "And not very well."

"*I'll* teach you." Lark wound almost a yard of thin, fine thread on to her spindle. "Sandry's coming along nicely…"

"I am?" asked the girl, eyes bright.

"You're learning to control magic *and* thread, and very well. Briar, *you* should lean straight spinning, no magic involved. And I should warn you, cotton and flax are harder to work with than wool."

"Will you teach me the spell you used on my waterspout?" asked Tris.

"It wasn't a spell," replied Lark. "I had no time to think of one."

"Then how'd you do it?" Tris demanded, puzzled.

Lark glanced at Niko, who put down his pen.

"Like yesterday," he said carefully, picking his words, "we see times when a mage doesn't know – or doesn't have time to think up – the right spell. When that happens, *open your mind.* Think of the objects and processes that you're comfortable with. That might be a spindle, waves, blows on an anvil, the growth of trees. Lark undid a waterspout. She had no spell for it, but she let her magic speak through her, and it worked."

Tris shivered. "It's that simple? Magic's that simple?"

His thick black eyebrows snapped together in a frown. "Magic is *never* simple, Trisana. Working it this way has its dangers. It's crude and sloppy. It burns up power faster than the magic you take time with, and use with control."

"It didn't hurt Lark," Briar objected. "Did it?" he asked her.

Lark smiled. "You learn better ways to handle it, as you study."

"I *don't* want you trying experiments with it," Niko said forbiddingly. "Magic is not your toy. I tell you this only because you might end up in a situation where you are forced to act fast." He returned to his letter.

After a moment, when it was clear that he was done talking, Tris asked Lark, "Would you teach me spinning anyway? Just in case?"

"If you want to learn, I'll teach you," replied Lark. "Daja? Are you interested?"

"If it doesn't get into my time with Frostpine."

"I wouldn't dream of taking you from him." Lark stared

into the distance, thoughtfully. "This time of day will be good for lessons, I think. And once you get the hang of it, the work is soothing."

"I give up," Briar announced with a sigh, putting his wool aside. "I hope I do better with plants for spinning."

"Having a spindle helps." Sandry crouched beside him, peering at a patch of wool on his shirt front. Pinching her fingers together, she pulled her hand towards her. "Come on," she ordered the wool. "Don't make me get stern with you."

"Hey! That tickles!" Briar cried as the fibres on his shirt wriggled.

"You can't feel the wool," she retorted.

"I can feel what you're doing to it, and it *tickles.*"

"Hold still," she ordered. Again she pinched her fingers together and drew them towards her. The loose fibres slowly pulled themselves together into a bunch.

The girl frowned. She *almost* had it. How had it worked the other day? The feeling had been a familiar one. Searching her memory, she had it: when her power did what she asked, it felt the same as if she had set a hard embroidery stitch, and her needle had darted through the cloth to lock it down perfectly.

Taking a breath, she found that same feeling inside, pinched, and pulled. The wool drifted over the gap between her and Briar, and landed on the hand she had beckoned with. Sandry looked at it, and beamed.

"Good," said Briar. He didn't realize that she had just done her first piece of deliberate magic. "Now can you get this bit on my britches?"

After that, their lives took on a pattern. Meditation, taught by Niko, came after morning chores. Sometimes they worked in the cottage, but he also took them on to the wall around Winding Circle, to the cave in the cliff, even to the garrets of the loomhouses, where the beat of working looms drummed through the timbers. Individual lessons filled the afternoons. In the evenings, the four read, studied, or worked at spinning. Lark was always present for that. At least one of the other teachers would come, to spin their own projects – Frostpine spun wire from silver, gold or copper – or tell stories, or teach something new. Those lessons weren't always magical: as the Willow Moon waned, Lark taught them all, even Tris, how to do handstands. In the month of Hawthorn Moon, Rosethorn showed them how to make a lotion to prevent sunburn. By then, the children needed it.

Midsummer was on its way; by the end of Willow Moon, the weather turned hot, and most adults preferred to stay indoors and nap after midday. If they weren't fighting – and fights often came up between Tris, Briar and Daja – the four lazed on their home's thatched roof, wearing broad-brimmed hats and sunburn ointment. Little Bear, denied the chance to follow them on to the thatch, waited below, looking mournful and abandoned.

Their teachers worked them hard. Rosethorn guided Briar in what he felt was an endless round of weeding, weeding, weeding. "It's early summer," she said when he complained. "Of *course* it's weeding, weeding, weeding."

As they worked, she told him about each plant: whether it was a flower, weed, fruit or vegetable; how he could recognize it, what uses it had in medicine, cookery and magic, if any. He was expected to memorize it all for those times when, out of nowhere, she would ask him to find a certain plant and tell her about it.

"I wake in the night muttering stuff like 'fennel'," Briar complained one day on the roof. "'None in the vegetable garden – most vegetables hate it. As a tea it is given to babies to relieve colic.' What's colic, please?"

The girls just stared at him. "It's a thing babies get," Daja said at last.

Briar made a face at her. "Where was I? 'Good for wrinkles, indigestion, helps to move the bowels. Also helps mothers produce more breast milk.'"

"*Breast milk?*" repeated Sandry, blue eyes wide.

"That's what she said. Then there's 'Grown around the home, fennel gives magical protection; hung in windows and doors, it wards off evil spirits.'"

"How can you be expected to remember all that?" Tris wanted to know.

"He just did," Daja murmured, watching little clouds grow into big ones.

"It's Rosethorn," Briar replied. "Believe me, if she told *you* to remember something, you'd remember it – or she'd want to know why."

No one argued with this. Weeks of acquaintance with the tart-tongued dedicate had filled them all with solid respect.

"What about you, *trangshi*?" the boy asked Daja, tickling the back of Sandry's neck with a straw. When Sandry turned to look at him, the straw was in his mouth, and he was staring at the sky. "What's that Frostpine teaching you?"

"What does that mean?" Tris asked. "No one's ever said. That '*trang*...'"

"The others speak Tradertalk, why can't you?" growled Daja. "It's *trangshi*, all right? It means..."

"Forbidden," offered Sandry.

"Bad luck," Briar said at the same time.

Tris eyed Daja. "What could you do at your age to be called that?" For a moment she thought the Trader might refuse. At last, in a few short sentences, Daja told her about the loss first of her ship, and then of her people. When she finished, Tris shook her head. For the first time, she felt sympathy for Daja.

"Maybe she doesn't like to hear that name, Briar," Sandry commented tartly, banging the boy's ankle with her fist.

Daja flapped a hand. "I don't mind," she said lazily. "Not from him."

"Because what a *kaq* says means nothing, right?" Briar asked. When Sandry looked away, he tickled the back of her neck again. She whirled, and glared at him.

"That's right," Daja said agreeably.

"So what does Frostpine teach *you*?" demanded Briar.

Daja sighed. "Lately he teaches me about coal. Coal's very important to a smith. He wants me to know how it's mined. 'Why does a smith have to know mining?' I ask him, and he just says 'You tell me.' At least I finally learned what all the basic tools are for. Now he's teaching me to make them. All of them. And put my magic into them."

"How goes it?" Briar wanted to know.

"Don't ask," Daja replied, glum. She looked at Tris. "What are your lessons?"

Tris sighed. "I learn the names of stars, and the words for different kinds of cloud, and keep a record of the tides. Weather stuff. Sky stuff."

"Tides aren't weather," Briar said.

"In the sea they are," replied Tris. "They're like winds, only in the water."

Scratching her shoulder, Sandry turned away from the boy. In a flash he leaned forward and brushed her neck with the straw. The scratching hand lifted; Sandry pinched her fingers together, and tugged. The straw leaped from Briar's hold, and went to her. She turned, blue eyes business-like, and flapped the hand that held the straw. The bit of grass flew at Briar's face. He shrieked, and covered his eyes with his arms. Undaunted, the straw hopped from his nose to his ears, tickling him mercilessly.

Forgetting where he was, Briar tried to scoot away. Before he reached the roof's edge, Sandry dropped the straw and grabbed one of his arms. Daja seized the other.

"Now *stop* it," Sandry ordered when the boy was settled again.

"Did you know you could do that?" asked Briar, grey-green eyes shining with admiration. "Yours is with thread, you told us."

"Well, you can weave straw, kind of. Next time, I'll see if I can unravel the string on your breeches if you don't leave me alone!"

The clock chimed the hour, making the air shiver. With groans, the four got up, and headed back into the cottage.

Midsummer's Day approached, and Winding Circle prepared for the holiday. The four helped to lay bonfires at the gates, and were kidnapped by the Earth temple's chief dedicate, to help scrub the temple floors. Wonderful smells lay in banks around the Hub as Dedicate Gorse and his cooks prepared a feast, and in lesser billows at the smaller kitchens scattered throughout the temple community.

Those odours had more power over Briar than even his lessons. He was late to the garden every day for a week, often arriving with stains on his shirt or smears around his mouth to betray where he'd been. Two days before the solstice,

Rosethorn tracked him to the Hub itself. Gripping one of his ears, she marched him away from Gorse's lair.

"But there was this *tremendous* smell!" he protested. "Like the spices you want me to memorize. I knew if I saw them being used, I'd learn them better. I was doing it for you – ow!" She had given his ear an extra twist.

"No humbuggery from you, my lad," she relied as she pulled him along. "Green Man wrap us, you'd think we never fed you!"

"You do! You do! It's just—"

She turned him to face her, and gripped his shoulders. "I don't know what's to become of you," she informed him, brown eyes fixed on his. "You may grow to be a true earth-mage. Maybe you'll join a temple; you might be the most sought-after gardener north of the Pebbled Sea. *That's* up to you. One thing is certain – hunger is a thing of the past. You may skip a meal or two, but you'll never starve. Take my word for that, and don't make me come after you again."

Suddenly he wrapped his arms around her, squeezed, and let go – then set off towards Discipline. Rosethorn, her cheeks red, followed him.

The day before Midsummer, Tris woke near dawn, full of restless energy. Since the day Niko had brought it up, she had wanted to try something. It was an itch that grew as she studied tides and winds, until it was more than she could stand. With their stretch of coast recently cleared of pirates, and preparations for the holiday going on, the watch on the temple gates would not be as sharp as usual. She could experiment now, before her housemates rose.

Dressing hurriedly, she slipped downstairs. Little Bear came out of Sandry's room as she passed, and whined. Outside, when she turned to latch the gate behind her, the pup was there. "If you come, be *quiet*," she ordered in a whisper.

Silently the dog followed. A few people were opening shutters and doors, but the spiral road was empty. The guards at the south gate had opened it for a wagon driven by a sleepy-looking novice. While they talked, Tris and Little Bear slipped through the open gate and across the road. They climbed down the trail, past the meditation cave, until they got to the beach.

The rock shelves on both sides of the cove were bare of water, showing seaweed, mussel beds and tide pools. Now at its lowest point, the tide had just begun to turn. By noon all but the tiniest sliver of beach would be covered in seawater.

"Let's see how good I am," the girl told Little Bear, sitting on a rock at the foot of the trail. The pup sat down as well, and yawned.

Closing her eyes, Tris started her meditation breathing, listening for the voice of her magic. In the weeks since beginning her studies, she had learned how to take strength from currents in the air or sea, if she were tired. She thought she could use that same magic to keep the tide from coming in, by pulling its strength into herself, or through herself, at least. The rock she chose as a seat looked like a good place to store the rest of it, until she chose to set that power free.

As a wave arrived, she called to its strength, taking it in. Without letting it go, she reached for the power of the next wave, and the next, draining the tide of force as it tried to cover the shore. With her eyes closed, she couldn't see that the water now lurked around the far ends of the rock shelves, bubbling and churning like a pot on the boil.

She grasped as much power as she could stand – to her surprise, she couldn't hold nearly as much of it as she had expected to. Like a sailor trying to empty out a sinking boat, she hurried to dump the strength from other waves into the rock beneath her. The sea fought hard, surging and pulling on her magic, trying to shake her loose.

Just a little longer, she thought. *Just a bit more, so I know I really did it…*

When Tris opened her eyes, the first thing she saw was Niko's face. "Uh-oh," she whispered, and closed them again.

"Now you know why one in ten Trader wind-mages lives to adulthood," that clipped voice said.

She tried to sit up. The rock under her felt strange – hardly like stone at all. For one thing, she'd had to crawl on to it; now she could just step off, once she had the strength. For another, it gave, more like a sack of grain than a proper boulder.

When she tried to lever herself off the stone with both hands, it collapsed, dropping her amid a shower of gravel, shattered into a thousand small pieces. Tris rolled on to her back, staring up at Niko. Little Bear came over, and licked her face.

"What happened to my rock?" she demanded lazily. "It's all to bits."

"It's where you placed what you took from the tides, isn't it?"

She nodded.

"You put in more than the stone could hold. It's dissolving. Now, let me ask – have you had a lesson today?" enquired the mage.

"You look very tall from down here," Tris remarked. His eyebrows came together in a scowl. Hurriedly she said, "When my teacher tells me it's a bad idea to try and fight the power of nature, I should listen."

He grasped her hands. "I don't know that I can walk," she admitted as Niko helped her to rise.

"I know very well that you can't," he said. "Your luck is in. The moment I knew you were in trouble, I enlisted a friend."

"Hello," Kirel said. Tris hadn't seen him waiting on the path. "You must be Daja's friend – the crotchety one." Grinning, he knelt, folded her over his shoulder and stood.

"This is so humiliating," grumbled Tris. She was too weak even to struggle.

"Let's go," Niko said. Little Bear, yapping with pleasure, danced around them as they began the long climb back home.

Winding Circle kept the Midsummer holiday in style, with a feast, music, dancing and rituals. One and all thanked the sun for its gifts on the longest day of the year, and prayed for a good harvest. Freed for the holiday, Briar, Sandry and Daja wandered through Winding Circle, listened to music, and ate until even Briar could not find a spare corner in which to lodge another bite of meat or cake. Tris remained at Discipline. Her experiment with tides had left her weaker than an overboiled noodle. She slept in the chair; when she lay flat and closed her eyes, the tide dragged at her bones, trying to pull her out to sea or dash her against rocks.

Little Bear kept her company all day. Now and then someone would look in – the other children, or one of the dedicates. Niko came by, and gave her a book called *Daring the Wheel: Those Who Defied Nature's Magic.* Reading it was a sobering experience for Tris. She had got off lightly; she was still alive.

As the longest day of the year drew slowly down to night, her stomach began to roll. Her pulse thumped in her ears; her feet and hands tingled. She fought to stand, trying to get a body no stronger than soup to carry her through a door a few feet away. Little Bear whimpered and circled her, barking, as she gave up on standing and crawled.

She had reached the outside doorstep when the ground shuddered, and flexed. Little Bear raced to the outdoor shelf that held Briar's *shakkan*, barking madly: the tremor had made it slide forward. Gulping against the need to vomit, Tris realized that yet another shake was on its way.

There was no time to think. She scrambled for the shelf as the *shakkan* leaped towards her, thrown off its support by the new tremor. With a yelp, Tris caught it, and held it steady. Little Bear whined, and tried to crawl into her lap underneath it.

Briar was the first to reach Discipline, at a run; Rosethorn was not far behind him. When they came through the gate, they stopped to stare. Tris leaned against the cottage, asleep. The *shakkan* was in her lap; Little Bear was draped over her shins. The new shelf on Briar's window hung only by one strut – the other had broken in the second tremor.

Tris woke as Briar lifted his treasure out of her lap. Guessing what caused his scowl, she said, "Don't thank me. You'll just scare me worse than I've been already."

Instead he reached his free hand down to her. "C'mon, old lady," he said. "Time to hobble inside." Rosethorn took the girl's other hand. Between them, they helped Tris into the house.

CHAPTER TWELVE

Niko had just started the next day's meditation when someone knocked briskly on Discipline's front door. He frowned, and went to answer it himself.

"I'm sorry, Master Niko." The novice was gasping for breath. "They want you at the Hub, *now*."

"I'm teaching—"

"Honoured Moonstream said it can't wait."

"I'll take them, Niko," called Lark from her workroom.

Niko hesitated, then followed the novice out of the cottage.

He was absent the rest of that day – Tris, waiting for her afternoon's lesson, gave up and continued to read *Daring the Wheel.* The residents of Discipline had just settled down to the night's spinning when Niko returned. "Lark, Rosethorn, if I may have a word?" he said, with a nod to the children.

They went outside, and talked so quietly that none of the four could eavesdrop, although they tried. At last the adults came back into the cottage, looking troubled.

"Come with me, Briar," Rosethorn ordered.

The boy carefully put down his spinning, and followed her to her workroom.

Niko gave another book to Tris. "Something's come up, and I am needed at the Hub for a while. Study this – it's about weather patterns in Emelan and her neighbours, and how one kind of weather may spark another. Meditate daily, record the tides and the moon's phases as I requested, and do whatever Lark and Rosethorn say. I'll look in on you as I can."

"Niko, what's going on?" enquired Sandry.

"I don't know yet," he replied. "That's the problem. There's all kinds of activity in the seeing and hearing places of the Hub – omens and portents are being reported from around the Pebbled Sea. We must sort through all that is being foretold, and try to put together the alternatives we are being shown."

"I don't understand," complained Daja, winding newly-spun thread on to her spindle.

With a sigh, Niko sat on a chair. "When seers view the future, it isn't a lone, solid image. The various choices that people make change any one future into many. Each choice in those futures gives birth to still more. Omens and visions are pictures from all those futures. Our task is to find the single event, or events, that started them. Once we find it, we can learn where that event takes place and when, and try to prepare."

"That sounds like work, if you ask me," Daja said firmly.

Niko smiled. "It is."

Rosethorn and Briar returned, the boy carrying a basket full of packets of herbs and bottles of liquid that Rosethorn had just measured out of her supplies. "I labelled everything," Rosethorn explained. "If they need more, tell them to send to me." Her mouth twisted wryly, and she added, "Perhaps mention that Crane's keep-awake tea is a *hair* better than mine."

Everyone stared at her.

"But *just* a hair!" she said crossly. "And *don't* tell Crane I said it!"

"I wouldn't dream of it," Niko reassured her, taking the basket. "Dedicates, thank you. Children, I hope to see you all soon."

"Mila bless," Lark said gently. "May the knot come undone and the threads be laid out straight for you to see."

Sandry blinked: as Lark spoke, the girl saw golden strands of power drift through the air, and twine gently around the mage. The other three sensed the magic's passing, and shivered.

Niko bowed, and left. The dedicates, and the children, drew the gods-circle on their chests, and returned to their work.

Over the next two weeks, whenever any of them saw Niko, his thick, black eyebrows were knitted in a thoughtful frown. He gave Tris more books and scrolls to work from. For several days he turned her over to Frostpine, who taught her and Daja the properties of metals. Niko rarely visited the cottage for meals; Briar was left to bathe on his own most nights. Even when Niko came to eat or teach, he was easily distracted.

Standing on the temple's northern wall with the others one hot afternoon, Daja saw a cloud billow from the windows of the Hub. "Is that—?" she asked Briar.

"The bird-cote," he replied. "It surely is."

The cloud of messenger birds broke up and spread, headed in all directions. Less than half an hour later, mounted couriers galloped out of Winding Circle.

"Something big," Tris remarked.

"Maybe someday they'll tell us what's going on," grumbled Briar. "That would be nice."

Two nights later, Niko joined them for supper. He looked

worn out. His eyes were puffy and bloodshot; the lines that framed his nose and mouth were deeper than usual.

"I *think* we've done all we can," he announced. "They got the word in time, certainly, and the message has gone to the coast cities and to the islands. Now all we can do is wait."

"What message?" asked Sandry.

"You're going to tell us what's up?" Briar wanted to know.

The man nodded. "Ragat will have an earthquake tomorrow, sometime before noon. Word's been sent to Ragat and her neighbour Pajun to prepare, and to everyone on the surrounding coasts who might be hit by a tidal wave."

"A quake? Are *we* in danger?" asked Tris, nervously.

"None. If there's a wave, the east shore of the Emelan peninsula will take the brunt of it, not our side," Niko told her. "Ragat is too far away for us to feel the quake itself." His fingers tapped restlessly on the table.

"Something bothers you still?" Lark wanted to know. "You can only alert people. It's not as if you can actually *stop* an earthquake."

"Why shouldn't they stop an earthquake?" Sandry asked when Niko didn't answer right away.

Tris turned suddenly pale; for a moment, she felt the power of the tides squeeze her. "Don't even *think* of such a thing!"

"It's a question of the power of the quake," Rosethorn pointed out. "It builds up over years. That power must go somewhere – you can't make it vanish."

"But there've been little shakes all summer," protested Briar. "Didn't that bleed some of it off?"

"No. They just made it stronger, because they weren't in the spot where *this* quake is growing. Am I right?" Tris asked Niko.

He nodded, and moved food around on his plate. "I don't

like the messages from Wave Circle Temple in Ragat," he said at last.

"Who's in charge there?" asked Lark.

"Honoured Huath," Niko replied.

Lark whistled softly. "Huath. Him and his machines, the ones that turn one kind of magic into another. What was the last one? Oh, yes – a mill that was supposed to turn the wind-magic into lightning-magic. How could I forget?"

"Did Huath say anything?" asked Rosethorn.

"His message to Moonstream, was, 'You may be surprised,'" Niko told her. "I don't like the sound of that."

"There's nothing you can do now," Rosethorn pointed out. "You look like you should be in bed."

"Even *Huath* isn't so prideful as to fiddle with an earthquake," Lark added, but the four heard uncertainty in her voice.

Niko sighed. "Tris, be patient for two or three more days. I've been leaving you on your own, and I know you need training badly. I *am* sorry, but a problem like this would take the sap from a far younger tree than I am."

"Is he allowed to talk like you do?" Briar asked Rosethorn. "About being a tree?"

Niko smiled. "Forgive me, Tris. I'll make it up to you." He levered himself to his feet, and left the cottage.

"Why's he tired?" asked Sandry.

"He's been far-seeing in his crystal, scrying for the future. It drains him," Lark explained. "We're lucky he was here to assist our own seers in sorting out the different omens." She got to her feet. "Who's got dishes?"

Was she dreaming? It looked so real, in places:

A woman, a maidservant by her clothes, sat on the

checkered tile floor, drinking from a heavy crystal decanter. The white sores on her face, arms and legs oozed; she couldn't open one eye at all.

"Have a drink wi' me, y'r ladyship," she said with a sly grin. "Drink t' Lord Death, as has us all."

"No, thank you," she whispered. Dodging the woman, she ran on as drunken laughter followed her. Her parents were here in this palace where empty corridors twisted and turned. Her mother, her father, Pirisi – she had to find them. It was time to go. She had never liked palaces. They were cold places, boxes of marble, crystal, metal and porcelain, with no place where a person could sit and be comfortable. Once she found her people, they could leave.

She stumbled around a corner, and was suddenly in her parents' bedroom. Here they were, still abed, as usual, arms wrapped around each other, as usual. Now they would sit up, and laugh, and beckon for her to come to them.

But they did not. She went to where they rested on the pillows, and shook her father's shoulder. He slipped down. She saw his face, the pockmarks dry and clotted, the white matter gone brown. Suddenly the reek of old death billowed over her, the smell of rotten meat. Her mother slid with him, locked to his chest, as dead as he was. Pirisi lay across the foot of their bed, her face battered by her murderers' attack. Her scarlet dress – mourning for her three children who died two days before – was unmarked.

A door slammed. She looked around, frantic.

The candles and lamps in the room went out. She was alone, in the dark, with the dead.

Sandry gasped, and sat up. The first things she saw were Discipline's white stone walls, and her embroidered Tree of Life hanging. It was almost dawn. There was plenty of light in the room; just as well, because her small bedside lamp was out. She frowned at it. Had the nightmare come because her light was gone? Perhaps she ought to ask Lark for a bigger lamp, if this one could run out of oil in one night.

Shaking, she got out of bed. The dream was always the same. Her parents looked just as they had when she found them. In reality, Pirisi had been alive, had been trying to stop her from entering their bedroom. In reality, they had heard the roar of the mob, and Pirisi had insisted on hiding her.

Pouring cold water into her basin, she scrubbed the fear-sweat off her face. Cleaning her teeth with hands that still trembled, Sandry vowed to ask Lark for a bigger lamp. She just had to stay out of the dark, that was all.

Everyone woke to a hazy sky and odd, orange-coloured light. The air was hot, damp and close. Little Bear ran from the front door to the back, whining. Tris had a headache, and a queasy stomach. Rosethorn and Briar were edgy. Daja, who liked to go barefoot when she could, put her shoes on. She was fine upstairs, but the ground outside the cottage seemed hot.

No one did well as they meditated that morning. They were all too restless.

"You'd better take a holiday, Briar," Rosethorn said at midday. "I'm going to lie down." Ashen, she went into her room and closed the door.

"I'll clean up," Lark said. She too looked unwell. "I need something to do. Go play – and take the Bear with you. He's annoying me."

Sandry hung her workbag off one shoulder, and caught the pup. She needed both arms to hold him. He was not as easy to carry as he was five weeks before, when they brought him back from the city. "Tris, maybe *you* should lie down," she suggested.

"She's right," Daja said. "You look like old cheese."

"Thanks ever so," Tris retorted, her voice dry. "Let's walk. Outside the wall if we can."

"Let's," said Briar. "It's not like *we'll* get that earthquake, or a tidal wave. Niko said we wouldn't."

Outside the gardens, Sandry let the pup go. He led the way through the south gate, shying at weeds and sniffing at pebbles. Suddenly he froze. A mouse nibbled on seeds in the grass between the road and the cliff. The four saw it just as Little Bear did.

"No!" yelled Briar, lunging at their pet. The mouse bolted, the dog in hot pursuit. Yelling for him to stop, the four gave chase, over the road, down the path, and into the cave. Little Bear kept going, into the depths of the cliff. His yapping struck echoes from the stone.

"I will skin that animal," Daja said, hunting for the lantern she had brought here weeks ago. She found it.

"We need to catch him first," grumbled Briar. "Little Bear, get your behind back here!"

Fumbling with the flint and steel kept beside the lamp, Daja struggled to produce a spark. Finally, the wick sputtered, then flamed.

Tris noticed that Sandry was staring at the lamp. "Are you all right? We have to go find him."

"I'm fine," replied Sandry, her voice harsh.

They followed the pup deeper into the cave, where they'd never gone before. The light, reflected from polished brass behind the wick, ran across lumps and curves in the cave, without touching a rear wall. They'd never realized the cave was so deep.

"We're *sure* about the quake and the tidal wave?" whispered Tris. The others looked at her. "I don't feel well."

"Niko was *positive* they wouldn't reach us," Briar insisted. "Stop worrying. Little Bear, come back here!"

Daja halted. Something in the wall caught her eye, a shiny layer in a bed of clay. "Sandry, take the lamp?"

"All right."

Daja handed the lamp over, and picked at the shiny material with a fingernail. "Trade winds' blessing," she remarked. "I wonder if Frostpine knows there's coal under the temple."

Briar came over, and laid his palm on the rock. Closing his eyes, he stroked it. "Rosethorn's right. It *is* made of really old plants," he said, awed.

On they walked, losing sight of the cave's opening when the tunnel curved to the left, and down. Daja kept one hand on the seam of coal. It broadened as they went deeper. "Why does the Fire temple pay high prices for Summersea fuel when we could start our own mine right here?"

"This whole place is like what's in my *shakkan*'s pot," Briar explained. "Rosethorn says when they built the temple in a crater, they put in pipes and layers of gravel and things like magic boundaries, so we don't flood when it rains. I bet they're scared to move anything underneath, high prices or no."

Little Bear galloped into their midst, tongue lolling, white showing all the way around his eyes. Sandry knelt to look at him, putting the lamp on the floor beside her. "Bear, what is it? What's wrong? He's shaking like a leaf," she told the others.

"Is he—" Daja began to say, and stopped. The warmth in the ground was burning through her shoes. Under her palm the wall heated so quickly that she yelped, and snatched her hand away.

"Don't look now," said Tris weakly, "but I think the tide's coming in. Again." She stumbled, and went to her knees. Little Bear howled, the air wailing as he set up echoes from the stone.

Briar gasped, pressing his hands over his ears. There was *screaming* in the ground, green voices shrilling their agony—

The floor jumped – or rather, it tossed them up, like toys on a sheet. A falling chunk of slate crushed the lamp. With a cry, Sandry collapsed on top of Little Bear. Daja leaped to help her; staggering as the floor pitched, she fell over Sandry and the dog.

The ceiling dropped, halting only inches over their heads.

The ground rolled, heaved and twisted for what seemed like for ever. At last it slowed, and stopped. For a moment there was nothing to hear but the grate of stone, Little Bear's whimper, and four throats, that rasped with each breath.

"It's dark." There was a shudder in Sandry's voice. "Don't leave me in the dark, please! I'll be good—"

"*Saati*," Daja croaked, tears rolling down her cheeks, "please don't talk like that." Something pressed on her back. She was arched, palms and feet holding her off the ground. Little Bear and Sandry were jammed under her belly, holding her up and being shielded by her. The long shaft of Sandry's drop spindle was digging into her breastbone. "What has happened?" asked Daja. "What's on top of us?"

Cloth rustled; gravel rolled. A questing hand almost hit Daja in the eye. "Sorry," Briar said. "Black as pitch..." He groped the surface at Daja's back.

"The dark," whispered Sandry. "Not the dark!"

Tris felt the area around her. "I have two big rocks here," she said. "One's at an angle. It keeps anything else from dropping on me from overhead – for now, anyway."

"Feels like coal on top of you, Daja," said Briar. "I got dirt on one side of me, and rock on another."

A hand felt around Daja's wrists. "Just me," Tris said. "Little Bear, c'mere." The puppy yelped as she grabbed one of his legs and yanked. "Sorry," she muttered. Pulling gently, she dragged the dog over to her.

"Sandry, come on," Briar said. "Don't go to bits. We got to think of something *fast.* There's after-shocks, y'know. At least get out from under Daja."

"Where are you?" Sandry asked with a sniff. "I can't see any—"

She screamed when Briar touched her arm. The rasp of shifting dirt filled the air. "You *got* to calm down!" he whispered. "We're in tight and we need *all* our wits!"

" 'Stead of the half one you got, thief-boy?" drawled Daja.

To her surprise, Tris chuckled.

Sandry gripped Briar's hands. As he pulled, she wriggled out from under the Trader. With a sigh, Daja began to kneel – and felt the coal at her back shift. Quickly she pressed herself against it once more.

A hand touched her ribcage. "What's the matter?" demanded Briar. "Why don't you sit?"

"The ceiling moved when I tried to."

Sandry began to sob. A small hand plastered itself over her mouth. "What is the *matter* with you?" Tris demand softly, her own voice shaking. As panicked as she was, she couldn't stand to hear Sandry in terror. "You faced down Crane and bullies and a crowd of truly vexed merchants, so I *know* you're not a coward."

"It's too hard to explain," whispered Sandry when Tris took her hand away.

"This is stupid!" Briar snapped. "We're supposed to have magic, and look at us! I don't know anything that can help. What use to be a mage if that happens?"

Daja half-remembered something. "Hush," she ordered, "I need to think."

"We're in trouble," croaked Sandry, and giggled. Little Bear licked her face.

No one moved. All around them sounds went through the ground; shifting earth, cracking stone. Briar listened hard for the rumble of an after-shock, though what he could do if one came was anybody's guess.

"I don't see how even a strong girl like you can hold up rock," Tris said at last, wiping her face in her skirt. "Your magic might be helping."

"Hold it – remember what Niko said?" asked Briar. "Think of objects and the workings we know, and open up – let what we know shape the magic, if we don't have the right spells."

"Wait a minute," replied Daja. "Let me see what I can find."

Closing her eyes, she took a deep breath, and coughed. Briar slid under her, bracing her legs and belly with his own back. Daja was able to relax against him, without their roof moving. "Thanks," she croaked when she could breathe again.

Swallowing, she took a slow, deep breath. Letting it out, she forced other thoughts from her mind. Never mind that she was hardly comfortable, never mind her nose was filled with dust, never mind the ache in her wrists and ankles. Breathe in, and in, and in…

Safety, she thought, drifting in silence. *I'd like to be* safe *for a moment, for now. Protected. Shielded...*

As clearly as if she stood in her room, she could see the *suraku*, her survival box. There was the mark of Third Ship Kisubo, stamped on its leather-covered sides. There were the straps that held it together; inside lay the copper lining that kept its contents safe.

Safe, she thought, and opened to her magic. *Make us safe.*

Power rolled away from her, growing to include the others, spreading around the hollow, taking the shape that meant safety to Daja Kisubo. That power told her what was around them: layers of stone, coal, and metal ore, and the bright flecks that were starstone pieces. Her power flowed into those things, grain by grain, stone by stone, shaping itself as a box. It was solid, and yet it wasn't: a magical *suraku*. Reaching its limit, three feet beyond them in every direction, her magic wriggled like a cat making a dent in a favourite pillow. It settled, and firmed. The bond between Daja and the thing she had just made broke. They were separate, she and the living *suraku*.

"I think we're all right for now," she whispered. "I – I'm *pretty* sure I did something, but ... don't start asking what I did, merchant-girl, because I can't explain. We're protected for now. I think."

Tris reached with her own senses, and found the magical barrier. "Will it let me find an air-vent?" she asked, worried. Her throat felt dry and clogged. "If we don't get air here soon, we'll be in deep trouble."

"We are anyway," Briar pointed out.

Daja remembered the way the magic had passed through stone and metal. "I think it will," she said. "I'm pretty sure, anyway. Try it." To her magic, silently, she added, *Please?*

There was a crack between the stones in Tris's corner. Putting her hands flat on either side of it, she drew in a deep, deep breath, and let it go. Outside the magical box that enclosed them, small land-waves rippled – not tremors, but the movement of badly stacked dirt and stones. They needed to move and resettle. Nothing was balanced in this ground; it could all shift at any moment. Tris shuddered as she explored. The land-waves' power was different from the restlessness of the tide when she tried to halt it, but it was the same. She had to do something quick, before those waves built the power to break through Daja's spell.

Breathing in, she called them to a clogged break in the earth, and shooed them gently ahead. The crack widened as the land-waves rolled through, shifting dirt and stone to either side.

Sandry whimpered as their coal roof groaned.

"Daja?" whispered Briar. "That sounds creepy. Can't your magic stop it?"

"What I made is outside what's on top of us. It can't hold the roof up."

"Lemme have a look," offered the boy.

They waited. When Tris inhaled again, Daja and Briar followed suit. Once they had the rhythm of inhale, hold exhale, they reached into the coal, feeling a multitude of tiny layers, pressed hard together. Daja felt its promise of fire to come; Briar felt the smug pleasure of ancient plants that had managed to change themselves into something different.

What do you think, Daja? His inner voice felt/sounded like pine needles in her mind.

Push up, with your magic. To Briar she felt/sounded like hot coals. *I'll push up with mine.*

Together they breathed in, deep. Briar thought of a trowel,

tamping down earth, and thumped their roof briskly. Daja thought of a bellows, pulling it open all the way, to get the most air inside. The coal crunched, and shifted upward.

Sandry cried out, but the others were too deep into their power to hear. Tris, sorting more earth-waves to widen her airway, broke through the ground's surface in three places. Water poured down one; hurriedly she closed it with a shock wave and stone. The other two openings were good; she felt air trickle into the space.

"Let's try moving me," Daja whispered to Briar. He slid out from under her, tucking himself between Sandry and Tris. Little Bear huddled in Sandry's lap. Very, very carefully Daja let her knees bend. She knelt, listening. The slab of coal didn't move. With a relieved sigh, she re-arranged herself until she sat on the ground, hugging her knees.

"It's holding," she whispered. "And the protection outside is still there."

For a long moment none of them said a word. They listened, or prayed, or wept silently, not wanting the others to know. There was no trace of light in their refuge. Every sound was important, a promise that they might die yet, just as the feeling of someone else's side, or foot, or tail meant they were still alive.

"Y'know, Bag, I woulda swore you didn't have a scared bone in your body," Briar croaked at last.

"Well, now you know," replied Sandry. "I'm scared of the dark."

"Just now I couldn't argue," Briar told her. In spite of her fear, Sandry grinned. "Is it because of you being in that cellar, the first time you did magic?"

She nodded, then remembered that no one could see. "I – I'm sorry, everyone. I'll try to do better, but..." In spite of herself, she sniffed, lips trembling. "This is even worse than it was there. I had a little more room, for one thing."

"But they found you," Briar pointed out. "You were all right then."

"No," whispered Sandry. "They had to blindfold me. The light hurt so much that I screamed. For a long time I didn't want to do anything, not eat, not work, not breathe. I got better in most ways, but – I hate the dark. I have to have a lamp by my bed at night."

"I don't want to upset anyone," Tris said, fighting to sound calm. She was grateful they *couldn't* see each other; what she felt in the earth around them was making her sweat. "The stones are talking. I can't explain, so you just have to believe me. Something very big and bad is coming at us from a long way off. Can we—"

"Another quake?" interrupted Briar.

"Mostly a quake," Tris replied. "And – maybe this is odd, but – it feels like there's *magic* all wound up in it. We have some time, but it's coming. Daja, I'm not sure the thing you did for us will hold."

CHAPTER THIRTEEN

For a moment none of them spoke. It was overwhelming news.

"We'd better do something fast," Daja said. "It's that or die. Tris, can you try anything with what's coming? Can you turn it around, or stop it? No, forget I said to stop it. I know you can't."

"All that power has to go somewhere," Tris replied. "And there's magic in what's coming – that complicates things. I don't know what I'm doing with my own magic, let alone someone else's."

Daja sighed. "Look, we must *try*. I'll find metal—"

"Maybe I can get plants to help us," said Briar.

Three sets of lungs inhaled. Briar let his mind branch through the earth, feeling a million traces of green in the distance. He strained to reach them, and failed. Daja found traces of iron, copper and lead scattered through the soil. She called them together, hoping to make a metal cage around her box. They shuddered, wanting to obey, but unable to.

Daja opened her eyes, gasping. "I need heat," she said. "I can't shape metals till I run them through a forge. Where do I find such heat, or control it?"

"Fire the coal?" Briar asked.

Tris was ill. Tension grew in the stones as the wave of strange force thundered their way. Her stomach was protesting. *I can't throw up now!* she thought fiercely. "Don't burn the coal, unless you want us to go with it!" she snapped. "We can't use real fire. Below, where volcanoes are born – it's heat. It's the essence of fire. Daja, if you control that heat – if you keep it off the coal..."

"My box – our protection. It's outside the coal right on top of us, so that's safe. I can keep it from the rest of the coal in this ground – I hope," replied Daja, coughing. She inhaled, and sent her magic out with her exhale, reaching for the heat that Tris had described. Soon she came back. "I can't," she told them, trying not to think of time running out. "My reach won't go that far."

Tris sighed. "Mine can, but I don't know anything about iron."

"I need to reach far, too," Briar said. "I'm just missing the plants' roots." In spite of himself, his voice quivered. He was getting scared. "I wish there was a way we could combine this fancy magic stuff."

Sandy had listened, shame and terror filling her mind. She was letting her friends down, sitting by useless when they were in danger. It had been the same when Pirisi was killed. Would she let that happen again? Couldn't she help?

Daja and Briar both needed Tris, and Tris needed strength. *What a tangle of knots!* she thought.

She gasped. "Waitwaitwait! I think – I think..." She grubbed in her workbag, digging past rolags, scissors, skeins of finished yarn...

A packet met her fingers. She pulled the contents out: her first spun thread. She hooked a finger around the shaft of her spindle, and dragged it out as well.

"Are you still thinking?" Daja enquired.

"We need to help each other, right?" She put the spindle down, and gripped the thread. "I have a way to make us stronger. Daja, I'm passing you a string with four lumps in it. Take the first lump, hold it, and put some of you in it – your magic, your memories, I don't care what as long as it's *yours*, understand?"

"I think so," Daja said. A hand gripped her arm, and a coil of thread was pressed into her fingers. She found a lump close to the end, and hung on to it.

"Give the long end to Tris, who does the same thing with the second lump. Keep it in your hand! Briar gets the third lump, I'll get the last. When part of you is in it, ask the gods' blessing, and give it back to me. Quick, now!"

Daja gave her lump the memory of red-hot iron lying in her unprotected hands. The excitement of walking in a storm as winds and rain lashed her went into Tris's knot. Briar gave it the feeling of green things twining around his arms and legs. The four of them on the roof, talking as clouds bloomed overhead, was Sandry's contribution. Four pairs of lips murmured a prayer to a favourite god.

Briar eased Little Bear on to his lap, where the pup curled up obediently. "Don't you make water on me," the boy ordered. Little Bear sneezed, and thumped Briar's ankle with a wagging tail.

Quickly Sandry took the thread and fixed it to her spindle as her leader, just as she had been taught. She had no rolags to prepare, not for the kind of spinning she had in mind. "Join hands," she told the others. "Actually, Briar and Daja, grab my knees. I need both hands if I'm to spin our magic."

"Work fast," Tris warned. "Can't you hear the stones?" *She* could hear them, shrieking with the first touch of the trouble that thundered down on them from miles away. The noise made her teeth ache, and her nose and eyes run.

"Everybody, breathe," Daja ordered. She closed her eyes

and inhaled, holding Tris's left hand in her right, and resting her left hand on Sandry's knee. Tris gripped Daja's hand and Briar's, while the boy rested his right hand on Sandry's left knee.

Without knowing it, Sandry spoke magically, not aloud. *I'm going to spin*, she explained. She placed her drop spindle in the tiny clear space at the middle of their hollow. *Fibres by themselves are weak – so are we. Spin them together, and they become strong. I think the spindle will bring our powers together and strengthen us.*

Do it, thought Tris urgently. Now the others could sense a distant wave in the earth, rushing to swamp them. Sandry gripped the spindle-shaft. With a snap of the fingers, she twirled it to the right.

Now that her magic was focused, the spindle was as visible to Sandry as if she worked on the spiral road at noon; so were the bits of her friends that they had put into her lumpy thread. Gently she touched Briar with a magical hand, and drew out a slim green fibre. From Tris she drew a blue one, the colour of deep, fresh water. Daja's was the reddish orange of a hot coal fire. Her own was the honey colour of undyed silk and flax. Feeding them all between her thumb and index finger of her hand, she connected them to her leader.

There was no time to stand and work, or to halt and wind new thread around the shaft of the spindle. She wrapped the magic around the long shaft as it whirled, with a silent apology to Lark for not doing this correctly. As Tris had reminded her, time was running out. She gave the spindle another twirl, and focused on her work.

As the spindle turned, Daja reached again for the iron ore. She felt it in her magic's grip instantly, as Tris connected her to a molten river far, far below. Carefully, making sure that she used only as much iron and heat as she could control, Daja brought them together. The ore shimmered, and began to melt.

Briar, his range much longer now, reached to the earth's surface. There a beacon of green fire called to him, giving his power the strength to leap across a band of open air and through dead wood and glazed clay. He tangled himself in the roots of his *shakkan.*

The miniature tree was rich with magic – each wrinkle, twig and leaf soaked in it – as well as the strength of each person who cared for it, whether that person had been a mage or not. Storing that power over its long life, pressing it into its small form, the *shakkan* had made it grow. Now it offered its magic to Briar.

With that power in his voice, he called to the roots of every living plant he could sense, trees and grass, bushes, weeds, flowers, herbs. The roots came to his call, stretching through the special soils and drainage layers that lay under Winding Circle, finding gaps in the interwoven pipes and magics that protected the temple, until they found the hollow where their friend Briar sat.

Sandry joined him. Together they wove the roots loosely around the *suraku*, Sandry working with the thin, string-like tendrils, Briar with the heavier tree-roots. That done, the boy wrapped the *shakkan*'s magic around root and rootlet, protecting them from the molten stream of iron, copper and lead that Daja made.

The heat she brought to her metals baked into Daja's skin, drying and cracking it; her sweat burned in the cracks. A tremor struck the hollow, rocking. Heat, sting, movement; once more she was on a raft in the middle of the ocean, foodless, waterless, the last of her family alive. A whirlpool dragged at her, trying to pull her in.

All around her magical *suraku* she found mats of woven plant-roots. Now what? She dared not burn them with her liquid metals. There had to be a way to work her iron, lead and copper into their shell, without killing Briar's friends.

Through the roots, she saw light: the spindle, whirling as it pulled magic from the four shapes. It reminded her of the wire threads Frostpine spun...

Wire threads. Wire. Her magical fingers reached into the pool where her liquid metals combined, taking just a pinch of fluid between thumb and forefinger. For a drawplate, she used her other magical hand, thumb and forefinger overlapping to form a tiny opening. She fed liquid metal through the opening, then gripped it and drew.

This way I don't trip over my own feet, she thought, once she was done. Nearby was a crack in the ground that contained sea-water. She didn't even know if this three-metal wire could be made outside magic, any more than she knew if a salt-water bath was good for it. Instead she logged a prayer to Trader Koma and Bookkeeper Oti, and plunged her creation into the water. It boiled off in a flash, and the wire took on shifting colours and shadows. Tongue sticking out of the corner of her mouth, Daja too began to weave.

Heat flared; the roaring earth heated up. Sandry could smell her friends' sweat. Watching Tris shove a wave of settling earth so it yanked the fresh heat away from them, Sandry grabbed a drift of warmth for herself, and let her spindle drive it deep into the earth. Tris herded still more heat ahead of her, until it burst through pinholes at the bottom of the sea, fuelling plumes of steam.

The land shrieked as it twisted and bucked in a fresh

earthquake. None of them heard their own cries as their hollow shelter wrenched. The pain of crushed rock and soil ground into Tris. She thought that her skull was being crushed between millstones; her eyes and nose ran. She began to cough.

"You don't sound good, merchant-girl," whispered Daja when things quieted.

"Dust," Tris replied faintly.

"Briar, it's the coal," Daja said. "Help me press it some more."

Both of them forced their minds, and their magic, against the slab over Daja's head, using the power that Sandry continued to spin for them. Their own strength was beginning to give out. As the thread that she drew from her friends went pale, Sandry poured more of herself into the spin. Grabbing more heat from the soil, she forced it to become power, and slammed it into her spindle. "You're going to work," she said grimly. "You're going to work, or I'll know why."

"Spoken like a noble," gasped Briar.

The new magic that she gave them was raw stuff that boiled in their veins. With it Daja and the boy hammered the coal until it had no more dust to shed.

"Brace yourselves!" cried Tris. A new earthquake was almost on top of them. "Gods help us, I don't think we can ride this one out!"

Sandry twirled her spindle as the ground bellowed in fury. The plants, metal and the box that sheltered them all groaned; even the *shakkan* was strained past its limit. Airways closed. Stone heated up.

The coal over Daja's head began to burn. "Tris!" she cried, losing the power to speak mind-to-mind. "We need water here!"

The spindle faltered. The threads that connected them began to fade in Sandry's magical vision. The *shakkan* started to draw away from Briar – he clung to it with all his strength. Tris broke the others' grip on her hands, scrabbling for the water she sensed just outside her reach.

Strength roared into the spindle and out along the roots, wires and *suraku.* Power that everyone could see flowed into the thread that Sandry had made, turning it from thin cord into heavy rope. The new magic cupped the hollow, drawing in around it as a fisherman's net closed around his catch. White fire, water-like, streamed over the burning coal, and doused it.

The earth still grumbled, but now it was the sound of rocks being crushed against one another. The hollow was moving through the ground. Little Bear whimpered, and crawled into Daja's lap.

"Sandry?" asked Briar.

"We're all right," she whispered. "I just don't know..."

They stopped moving.

Daja's *suraku* evaporated. Dim voices reached their ears. Through a chink in the rock, Tris saw a patch of light grey. The new magic vanished; the spindle fell on its side with a clatter. Slowly, nervously, Briar and Daja let go of Sandry.

"No, idiot! You'll kill the roots!" A sharp, familiar voice penetrated the hollow. "Let me!"

"Then get it done, woman!"

"Rosethorn," whispered Briar, voice cracking. Root by root, he felt his plants draw away from the hollow under his teacher's gentle touch.

Frostpine, thought Daja, and sighed.

"Safe?" murmured Sandry, lips trembling. "We're *safe*?"

They couldn't see it, but they felt it. Power entered their

hollow, weaving to form a net under the coal. With a spattering of loose dirt, the roof of their hollow began to rise.

"Carefully," Tris heard Moonstream order. "We don't want accidents at this point."

Daja leaned against the wall and closed her eyes. Tears of exhaustion and relief trickled down her cheeks.

Blinking, the children shaded their eyes against flickering torchlight behind the ring of faces that looked down at them. They were in the Heartfire chamber of the Hub. Moonstream was there, hands tucked into her wide sleeves. So too were Niko, Lark, Rosethorn and Frostpine. The children knew few of the other initiates who had helped bring them from the earth, except for one.

"Dedicate Gorse!" croaked Briar. "Have you got anything to eat?"

None of the four made an easy recovery from the earthquake. In addition to the same weakness that kept Tris in bed after her experiment with tides, they were bruised from head to toe. Sandry's hands were crossed by red welts, as if she had tried to spin a hot wire.

At first they slept an entire day in Winding Circle's infirmary. Waking briefly, they swallowed clear soup, and slept again. It was night when they woke for the second time. The healers gave them fruit juices and herbal teas, making them drink every drop before allowing them to sleep again.

Tris woke around dawn. Niko helped her into a chair, while Lark placed her spectacles on her nose. By the time she had eaten a bowl of thin gruel, Briar, Sandry and Daja were awake. Even Briar didn't object to the gruel. It tasted wonderful. None of them left as much as a spoonful for Little

Bear, whose ivory curls had been washed and combed while they slept.

"We took damage," Lark explained, once all four had eaten. "It would be a miracle if we hadn't. Most of our people are in Summersea, though – that's where it hit hardest. Rosethorn and Frostpine are bringing survivors out of the ruins still, and it's been three days."

"Someone tried to stop the quake in Ragat, didn't they?" Tris's voice was little more than a croak.

"No, no, they didn't try to *stop* it," Niko protested, his voice very dry. "They *knew* it was folly to stop a quake. Honoured Huath and the Wave Circle mages wanted to *trap* it. They thought they could store it, as you might store power in a crystal, or a *shakkan*, for use later."

Little Bear yapped, sensing Briar's sudden anger.

Sandry blinked several times. "I could have sworn you just said they wanted to trap an earthquake."

"It gets better," Lark said, brushing the tangles from Sandry's hair. "As it bounced around the crystals they used to trap it, the quake got stronger. Finally it broke out of the holding spells, and went in *every* direction."

"Is this Huath going to get in trouble?" Sandry wanted to know, eyes blazing. "If the *temples* don't do something—"

"Huath is dead," Niko told her. "Him, and all of Wave Circle Temple."

Tris and Sandry made the gods-circle on their chest. Daja, about to spit on the floor with contempt, saw Lark watching, and changed her mind. Briar thought, *Better that Huath than us.*

Yes, chorused the girls, without realizing they'd spoken magically.

They felt well enough to visit the privy, though afterwards

all of them felt like a fresh nap. "Is this going to happen *every* time we use big magic?" Briar demanded, collapsing on to his cot.

Niko smiled. "The better you get, the less tiring any exercise of magic will be. I should mention, though, that it will be a long time before you can recover easily from the sort of magic you worked down there. I wouldn't have thought it possible with beginners."

"Sandry spun us, to make us stronger," Daja explained.

Niko shook his head. "When you feel better, we must sit down and get your story in full. You've already given a number of people much food for thought."

"My favourite activity," grumbled Tris, pulling her blankets over her shoulders.

"We'll have you home soon," Lark told the four. "At least you can look at walls you know." She kissed each of them on the forehead, and left with Niko.

We did *do pretty good for ourselves, didn't we?* Briar flopped back on to his pillow.

And if we're very, very lucky, we won't do so well for ourselves again, Daja retorted.

They were released the next day, and given a cart-ride to Discipline. They made it through the front door, but only barely. Tris and Daja were grateful to see that cots had been set up for them in the main room. Dosed with Rosethorn's herbs, breathing summer garden smells wafting through every door and window, the four felt much better. Within a day or so they began to straighten up the cottage. It had received a shaking. While nearly everything was in one piece, few of the pieces were where they were supposed to be.

The moment that she could manage it, Daja climbed the

stairs to her room. As she had thought, her altar had fallen over, scattering incense and images across the floor. Her box stood at the foot of her bed, looking as it always had. The first thing the Trader did was tend the *suraku*, polishing its metal and oiling the leather, until it gleamed.

"It saved me twice," she explained to her gods and ancestors as she set up her altar again. "I had to repay the debt." If they were displeased, they showed no sign of it. She didn't think they would be.

Sandry's first act, once home, was to put her green drop spindle on a shelf. Beside it she placed the thread with four lumps in it. It had somehow woven its loose ends together as she had spun it underground, and now it formed a ring. There was no way even to tell where the loose ends had met: the circle was complete, the four lumps equally spaced.

Once she was able to walk without feeling she would melt over the floor, she straightened Lark's workroom. Lark herself was at the loomhouses, to help mend the damage there. Cleaning up was pleasant work for Sandry, particularly since she was now able to call any unruly wool, silk, flax or cotton to order if it tried to misbehave.

Briar sought out his *shakkan* as soon as he returned to the cottage. It had taken no harm from the quake; the shallow dish was uncracked, the earth inside just as he'd left it. Putting his hands on the thick trunk to thank the tree, he now felt the power that had been hidden in it before, sunk deep in each fibre.

It also had buds at the end of each twig. "None of that," he warned, starting to pinch them off. "Your helping me doesn't mean I'll let you grow any which-way."

He felt something like a tree-sigh under his hands. The *shakkan* thought, *Perhaps* one *new bud*?

"Oh, all right," Briar said. "Which do you want to keep?"

The tree seen to, a few more meals and another night's sleep under his belt, Briar decided to have a look in Rosethorn's shop. She was still in Summersea, where her knowledge of medicines was desperately needed.

Dismayed by the mess in her workroom, Briar sorted through the packets and bottles strewn over the worktables and floor, and rescued the potted plants. Gathering up some labelled bottles, he went looking for Tris, and found her on the back stoop, bent over something in her lap. Power rose like a ghost around her; he felt it as he'd felt the magic in the balm Rosethorn had smeared on the children's bruises. "What are you doing?"

Tris squeaked in alarm and hid the thing in her lap. "Nothing."

"Come on, I could feel it. What have you got?"

"I *said*—"

He sat beside her. "I won't go till you tell." He put the bottles he'd been carrying by the door. Little Bear, who was exploring the garden, came to sit with them, scratching one of his own healing scrapes.

"It's nothing—"

"Don't lie to me, four-eyes. You're the worst liar in this house."

"I'm not lying, exactly," She sighed windily. "I'm just trying something, that's all." Looking at the bottles, she said, "Do you want me to teach you how to read?"

Although he wanted to ask just that, he bristled. "Who says I don't know how?"

The look she gave him was one of amused scorn. "Do you think I didn't notice you wait till you see what chores everyone else has before you start yours? I was *going* to offer."

"I wouldn't mind learning," he admitted. "I'll teach you how to fight, then."

She grinned. "I'd like that!"

"It's a bargain. Now, tell me what you're up to."

Turning red, she held out a round blob of smoke-grey crystal, filled with cracks and copper threads. "I thought I could put light in it. Frostpine says crystals are good for that, and they last for years. I'm weak as a kitten, though."

"For Sandry?" he asked quietly.

Tris nodded.

"Lemme see if I can help. Come on," he argued when she hesitated. "It's a good idea. Let's try. Breathe in..."

Together they inhaled, held the breath, let it out, clearing their minds as they exhaled. It was easier for both to do now. Once they were settled, Briar cupped the girl's hands in his, and they concentrated on the crystal.

"What are you doing?"

Occupied as they were, neither Briar nor Tris knew that Daja had come in search of them. They jumped, and pulled apart. "Nothing," they both said.

Daja sat cross-legged beside them. "Nonsense. I felt the magic clear upstairs."

"We just want our strength back, so we're meditating," Briar told her.

Scornfully, Daja held out her palm. Tris sighed, and handed the crystal over. Some of the breaks and threads now sparkled.

"For Sandry," Briar explained.

"So she'll always have a light," added Tris.

"You'd better let me help," Daja said. "Where did you find this, anyway?"

"It fell out of the coal when they rescued us," Tris said. "I just picked it up."

Daja put the stone in her cupped palms. Briar cradled her hands with his; Tris covered them. Three sets of lungs began a long steady breath.

Sandry woke when Lark went out for the Earth temple's midnight rites. About to go back to sleep, she saw a light under her closed door. Little Bear, curled up on her bed, jumped down and nudged the door open. In came Daja, Briar and Tris, all in their nightshirts. Daja offered her their unflickering light; stronger than Sandry's bedside lamp, it shone from the small, round crystal that she carried.

"So you never have to worry about the dark again," explained Tris.

Briar tossed her a small leather pouch. "See, if you put it in there, it doesn't show, and you can hang it around your neck."

Sandry, voiceless, took the crystal, holding it up before her eyes.

"Crystals can be spelled and hold power for a long time," Tris explained. "We figure—"

"We *hope*," Daja corrected.

"We *hope* that by the time the power leaves the crystal, you won't be afraid of the dark any more," Briar explained.

Sandry's eyes filled, and spilled over. "Thank you," she said. "I couldn't ask for better friends."

"Don't get all sloppy on us," retorted Briar. "Girls!"

Little Bear barked sharply. They had paid enough attention to their light and to Sandry; now they could pet him. Obedient to his orders, Daja scratched his ears, and Tris his rump.

About the author

Having worked as a housemother in a group home, a literary agent's assistant and an investment banking secretary, Tamora Pierce now writes for a living (with time off for school visits and book gatherings). She now has nine books in print, and is hard at work on three more.

New York City is her home. She shares it with her husband, technical writer Tim Liebe, their three cats, two budgies and whatever animals she rescues from affliction in the park.